D0578183

Civil War *and* Reconstruction

★ ★ ★ THE MAKING OF AMERICA ★ ★ ★

Civil War *and* Reconstruction

Michael Weber

RAINTREE STECK-VAUGHN PUBLISHERS
A Harcourt Company
Austin • New York
www.steck-vaughn.com

Copyright © 2001 Steck-Vaughn Company

All rights reserved. No part of this book may be reproduced or utilized in any form or by any means, electronic or mechanical, including photocopying, recording, or by any information storage and retrieval system, without permission in writing from the Publisher. Inquiries should be addressed to: Copyright Permissions, Steck-Vaughn Company, P.O. Box 26015, Austin, TX 78755

Published by Raintree Steck-Vaughn Publishers, an imprint of Steck-Vaughn Company

Developed by Discovery Books
Editor: Sabrina Crewe
Designer: Sabine Beaupré
Maps: Stefan Chabluk

Raintree Steck-Vaughn Publishers Staff
Publishing Director: Walter Kossmann
Art Director: Max Brinkmann
Editor: Shirley Shalit

Consultant Andrew Frank, California State University, Los Angeles

Library of Congress Cataloging-in-Publication Data
Weber, Michael, 1945-
Civil War and reconstruction / Michael Weber.
p. cm. -- (The making of America)
Includes bibliographical references (p.) and index.
ISBN 0-8172-5707-1
1. United States--History--Civil War, 1861-1865--Juvenile literature. 2.
Reconstruction--Juvenile literature. [1. United States--History--Civil War, 1861-1865. 2
Reconstruction.] I. Title. II. Making of America (Austin, Tex.)
E468.W42 2000
973.7--dc21

00-029061

Printed and bound in the United States of America
1 2 3 4 5 6 7 8 9 0 IP 05 04 03 02 01 00

Acknowledgments
Cover The Granger Collection; pp. 9, 11, 13 Corbis; p. 16 The Granger Collection; p. 18 Corbis; p. 20 The Granger Collection; pp. 22, 23, 25, 27 Corbis; p. 29 The Granger Collection; pp. 34, 35 Corbis; p. 37 The Granger Collection; pp. 39, 42, 45 Corbis; p. 47 The Granger Collection; pp. 48, 49 Corbis; p. 50 The Granger Collection; pp. 51, 52 Corbis; p. 54 The Granger Collection; pp. 55, 56, 58, 60, 62, 63, 64, 65, 67 Corbis; p. 70 The Granger Collection; p. 71 Corbis; p. 72 The Granger Collection; pp. 73, 74, 75 Corbis; pp. 76, 79 The Granger Collection; p. 80 Corbis; p. 82 The Granger Collection; p. 84 Corbis.

Cover illustration: This 1886 lithograph shows a scene from the Battle of Shiloh during the Civil War. The battle took place in Tennessee on April 6–7, 1862.

Contents

Introduction

By the 1800s, slavery had become deeply embedded in the Southern states of the United States of America. In the North, there was serious opposition to slavery because it contradicted the ideals of liberty and equality on which the United States had been founded. But successive generations of government leaders had failed to solve the problem, and the differences between North and South grew sharper.

Southerners saw slavery as an essential part of their way of life. They believed the preservation of slavery, and its spread into new U.S. territories in the West, was essential to their prosperity. And increasingly, Southerners feared that a powerful federal, or national, government might come under the control of those who wanted to restrict slavery and perhaps abolish it altogether. Ever since the Constitution had been written, there had been arguments about the balance of power between the national government and the states. Many Southerners believed in a political theory called "states' rights," which said that individual states should decide many issues for themselves, including whether or not they remained in the Union.

> "We have no [great] cities. We don't want them. . . . We want no manufactures; we desire no trading, no mechanical or manufacturing classes. As long as we have our rice, our sugar, our tobacco, and our cotton, we can command wealth to purchase all we want."
>
> *William Howard Russell,* My Diary North and South, *1861*

The conflicts about slavery and states' rights led Americans into a civil war, a war in which citizens of the same nation fight each other. The Civil War, which lasted from 1861 to 1865, produced scenes of both horror and bravery that have become legends in American history. During the war, more than a million people were killed or wounded and large areas of the country, mainly in the South, were devastated.

The Reconstruction years of 1865 to 1877 and the years beyond were also a period of terrible turmoil. During Reconstruction, the United States tried to rebuild its Southern states, and to make a new place in society for the huge black population recently freed from slavery.

1

The Dividing Nation

In many respects, the United States in the first half of the 1800s was a thriving, prosperous nation. The country had expanded greatly in size. The Louisiana Purchase of 1803 had doubled the land area of the United States. All or part of 15 future states were carved out of this vast region purchased from France. Other important areas were also acquired by purchase, negotiation, or war: Florida in 1819, Texas in 1845, the Oregon Territory in 1846, a vast area won from Mexico in 1848, and the Gadsden Purchase in 1854. These regions nearly doubled the land area of the United States again.

Growth in the 1800s

The country was changing, too. In 1800, the population of the United States was about 6 million people. By 1860, it had reached 31 million. In 1800, only six percent of the U.S. population lived in towns or cities of more than 2,500. But in 1860, 20 percent lived in towns or cities.

The white people of the United States, on the whole, were well educated. Their literacy rate—the proportion of the people who could read and write—was one of the highest in the world. Most people of the period earned their living from farming. New improvements and inventions—better plows, reapers, threshing machines, the cotton gin—contributed to greater farm production. Between 1820 and 1860, total farm output in America increased 400 percent.

Meanwhile, there was also a large increase in the number of workers engaged in manufacturing. Mass production of goods in factories began, and the output of the U.S. economy increased sevenfold between 1800 and 1860. Roads, canals, and railroads were being built at a tremendous rate. By 1860, the United States had as many miles of railroad track as the rest of the world combined.

Differences Between North and South

These trends and changes, however, did not take place to the same extent in all parts of the country. The North and South were very different. The North had a dynamic, forward-looking character. The South, in contrast, was much more bound by tradition. The population of the South was far less educated than that of the North. Black people in most Southern states were barred from receiving any education, and there was no system of public schools for whites as there was in the North.

The North and South in 1860

This table shows what huge differences there were between the North and the South in their economies and populations just before the beginning of Civil War. The figures for the South include 3,500,000 slaves.

	North	South
Total Population	22,700,000	9,000,000
Percentage of Population in Cities and Towns	26	10
Percentage of Children in School	72	35
Percentage of Weapons Manufactured in U.S.	97	3
Percentage of Cloth Manufactured in U.S.	94	6
Percentage of Iron Manufactured in U.S.	93	7
Percentage of Boots and Shoes Manufactured in U.S.	90	10
Acres of Farmland	105,000,000	57,000,000
Number of Factories	110,000	18,000
Number of Workers in Industry	1,300,000	110,000
Miles (km) of Railroad Track	22,000 (35,400 km)	9,000 (14,500 km)

In the South, the economy depended on slaves such as these working on a cotton plantation. Slaves grew three-quarters of all the cotton, half of the tobacco, and nearly all the rice and other crops.

The South also benefited less from the new developments in transportation and industry. There were fewer roads, canals, and railroads than in the North, and not nearly as many manufacturing industries. In 1860, New York and Pennsylvania each produced more than twice as many manufactured goods as all the 11 Southern states combined. The South got most of its manufactured goods from the Northern states or from Europe.

These goods were paid for with income from the sale of a few crops—especially cotton, rice, and tobacco—in markets in the North and around the world. By 1860, "King Cotton," as the cotton trade was known, accounted for half of all U.S. exports. But many of the merchants, shippers, and bankers who controlled the trade were Northerners. The South had few businesses of this kind, and Southerners greatly resented their dependence on these outsiders.

The biggest difference between North and South, of course, concerned slavery. Slavery was at the root of many of the other differences as well. By 1860, slavery had been abolished virtually everywhere in the North. But in the South, slaves made up half of the labor force. The prosperity of the plantations that grew cotton, tobacco, and food crops depended on the free labor of slaves. Slaves also performed

"Our whole commerce except a small fraction is in the hands of Northern men. Seven-eighths of our Bank Stock is owned by Northern men. . . . Financially we are more enslaved than our Negroes."

A resident of Mobile, Alabama, 1847

> "With us the two great divisions of society are not the rich and the poor, but white and black; and all the former, the poor as well as the rich, belong to the upper class, and are respected and treated as equals . . . and hence have a position and pride of character of which neither poverty nor misfortune can deprive them."
>
> *John C. Calhoun of South Carolina, 1848*

much of the non-agricultural work, such as mining, transportation, and what manufacturing there was.

Surprisingly, only one-third of white families in the South owned slaves. And half of those owned fewer than five slaves each. It was quite a small group of wealthy plantation owners—12 percent of all slaveholders—that owned more than half of all the slaves. Nevertheless, skin color served to unite most whites against blacks. Generally speaking, the poorest white people felt closer to the rich plantation owners than to black slaves or even to free blacks.

Abolitionists in the North

Meanwhile, antislavery feeling was growing in the North. By around 1830, the movement known as "abolitionism" had gained significant strength. The abolitionists hated slavery and wanted it ended immediately. Abolitionists were both men and women, and included whites and free blacks, including former slaves. Many were spurred by strong religious convictions. Abolitionists founded organizations dedicated to the abolition of slavery. They wrote books and pamphlets, gave lectures, and petitioned Congress.

Although they gained thousands of followers, abolitionists remained a minority in the North. In fact, many Northerners considered them to be dangerous troublemakers. After all, the Constitution protected slavery as a form of property ownership, and few whites thought black people were their equals. At times, mobs in the North destroyed abolitionists' printing presses and other property. These mobs were usually composed of poor workers who feared that ending slavery would result in freed slaves coming North and taking their jobs away.

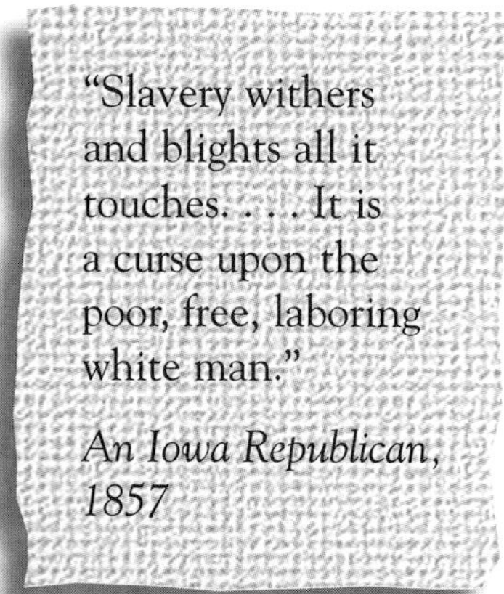

> "Slavery withers and blights all it touches. . . . It is a curse upon the poor, free, laboring white man."
>
> *An Iowa Republican, 1857*

Even so, many Northerners recognized that, in principle, slavery was wrong. They were willing to accept slavery where it already existed in the South, but they opposed its spread into new areas. In the 1840s, small antislavery political parties—the Liberty party and the Free-Soil party—were formed. Influenced by abolitionists, some Northerners came

Sojourner Truth (c.1797–1883)

Sojourner Truth was born in Ulster County, New York, the youngest daughter of two slaves who had either 10 or 12 children. Her original name was Isabella. Her owners were of Dutch ancestry, and she grew up speaking Dutch. When she was nine years old, Isabella was sold away from her family.

She lived with and worked for a farming family for 16 years. During those years, Isabella married and had five children. Several of her children were taken from her and sold by her owner.

In 1799, New York had passed a law to free its slaves by 1827. In that year, Isabella gained her freedom and settled in New York City. She had always been religious, believing she received direct communications from her own god. (Later, her beliefs moved closer to those of what is now the Pentecostal Church.) Isabella became a preacher at religious revival meetings. In 1843, she took the name Sojourner Truth, and believed she had been called by God to fight against slavery and for women's rights. Truth lectured for years all over the United States, drawing large crowds.

After the Civil War, Sojourner Truth worked for the Freedmen's Bureau in Virginia. She was appointed by Abraham Lincoln as counselor to the freed slaves of Washington, D.C. Truth also spoke in favor of creating a "negro state," and encouraged the United States government to give land in Kansas for black settlements there.

to believe that a vast conspiracy existed in the South to spread slavery into the western territories of the United States and even to conquer new lands where slavery could be established. Northerners sometimes referred to this conspiracy as the "Slave Power." For such Northerners, slavery was the enemy of a healthy, prosperous society.

Southerners Defend Slavery

Southerners, however, thought it was their society that was superior. In earlier years, some prominent Southerners, such as Thomas Jefferson, had expressed the hope that, some day, slavery could be ended. But the boom in cotton production changed things. By the mid-1800s, slaves were so essential to the Southern workforce that a society without them was impossible for many Southerners to imagine.

"Many in the South once believed that slavery was a moral and political evil. That folly and delusion are gone. We see it now in its true light, and regard it as the most safe and stable basis for free institutions in the world."

John C. Calhoun, 1838

Nine of America's first 15 presidents were Southern-born slaveholders and several other presidents were also sympathetic to the South. For most of the years between 1789 and 1861, Southerners were very powerful in national affairs. Nevertheless, many Southerners feared the power of the federal government.

Back in the 1790s, Thomas Jefferson and James Madison, both Virginians, had developed a theory of interpreting the Constitution called "states' rights." It stressed the importance of the powers of the states and said the powers of national government should be limited to those specifically mentioned in the Constitution. Jefferson and Madison believed a powerful federal government would take away the liberties of the people. States' rights became a key belief of the Democratic party, in which Southerners played a leading role. It also became the cry of Southerners determined to defend slavery.

As the 1800s progressed, more and more people in the South feared a strong federal government might take action against slavery. They imagined that behind every critical comment about slavery lay a plan to abolish it. Earlier, they had defended slavery as a necessary evil. Now, however,

In both North and South, people attacked abolitionists and their beliefs. This cartoon shows William Lloyd Garrison,(center) editor of the Liberator *antislavery newspaper, being mobbed by an angry crowd.*

Southerners spoke of slavery as a positive good. The Declaration of Independence was wrong, some Southern thinkers argued, and all men were not really created equal. They said slavery was justified by religion and the Bible. These people believed the different races of humanity varied in their ability, strength, and intelligence, and therefore slavery was good for both masters and slaves.

In 1831, a slave rebellion in Virginia led by Nat Turner had killed dozens of whites. Although large-scale violence by slaves was very unusual, Southerners began to take extreme measures to preserve order and prevent the spread of antislavery opinion. States enacted stiff penalties for speech or writing that might encourage discontent among slaves. Officials seized from the mail any materials they thought dangerous. Strangers, especially from the North, could find their movements watched and their luggage searched. Abolitionists and other outspoken critics of slavery might even put their lives at risk if they traveled in the South.

Disputes between North and South

The Missouri Compromise of 1820 kept the balance between slave and free states by admitting Maine as a free state when Missouri became a slave state. In 1850, a series of acts known together as the Compromise of 1850 was passed. Under these laws, California became a free state; Utah and New Mexico, with the right to make their own decisions on whether or not to allow slavery, became slave territories.

In the years from 1820 to 1861, a series of disputes increasingly divided North and South. At the heart of these disputes was the issue of slavery. The disputes mainly concerned whether slavery would be permitted in the new lands being settled in the West.

The first dispute arose in regard to Missouri. The Missouri Territory was part of the land the United States acquired in the 1803 Louisiana Purchase. Many of the settlers in Missouri had come from the South and had brought their slaves with them. In 1819, Missouri applied to Congress for admission as a state. At that time, there were 11 states where slavery existed and 11 where it did not. Since each state had two United States senators, the balance of power in the Senate between "slave" and "free" states was even. Missouri would tip the balance one way or the other.

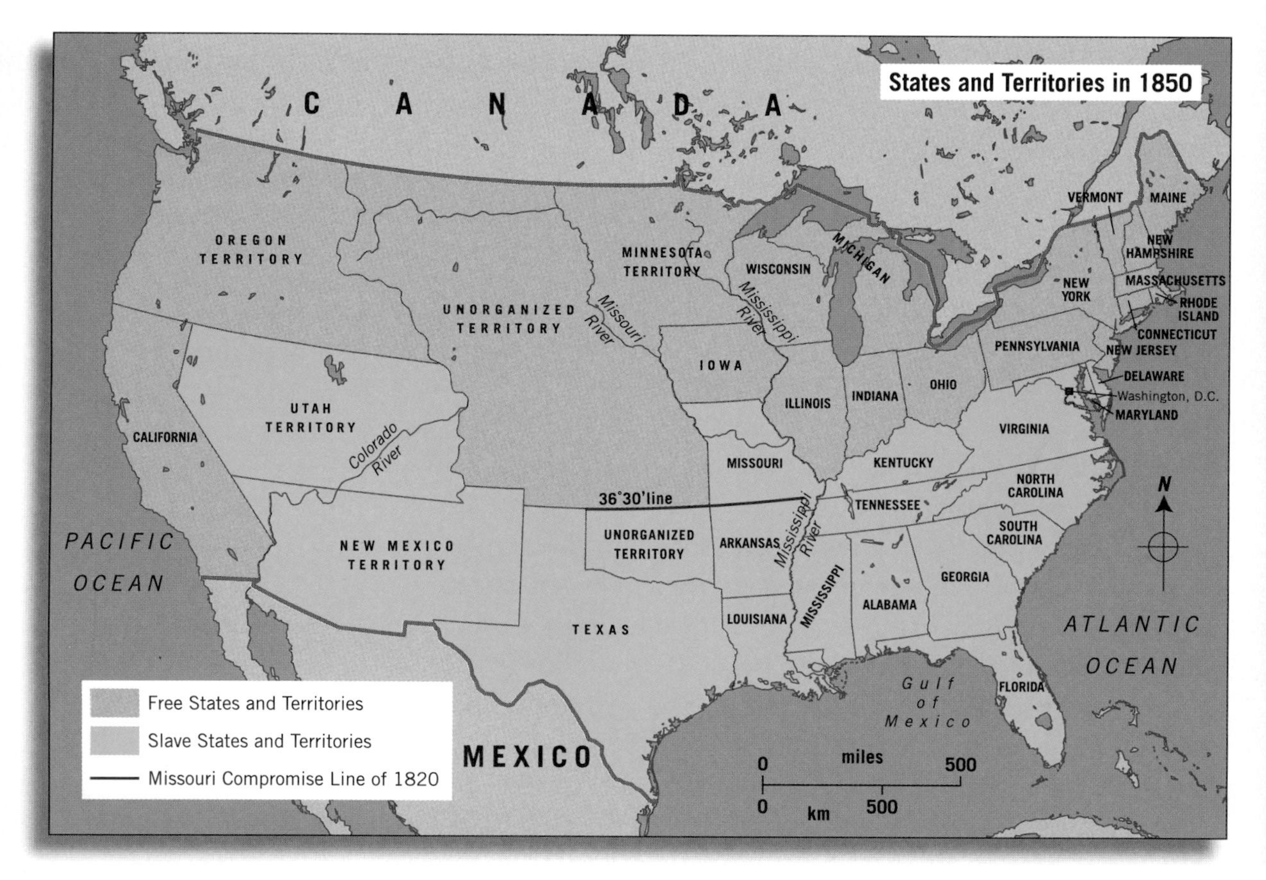

A New York congressman proposed that slavery be ended in Missouri after it became a state. For the first time, Congress debated whether it could regulate slavery and questioned the morality of slavery itself. In 1820, Representative Henry Clay from Kentucky helped work out the Missouri Compromise. Under this compromise, Congress admitted Missouri without any restriction on slavery. At the same time, it also admitted Maine as a free state. (Until then, Maine had been part of Massachusetts.) In this way, the balance between slave and free states was preserved. For the future, Congress prohibited slavery in the rest of the land of the Louisiana Purchase north of the 36°30' latitude line, the southern boundary of Missouri.

But the slavery problem returned again and again. The annexation of Texas was delayed in the 1830s and 1840s because of controversy over slavery. In 1848, the United States acquired large territories from Mexico in the Treaty of Guadalupe Hidalgo after the Mexican War. The area included the future states of California, New Mexico, Arizona, and Utah. Many Southerners hoped that slavery would flourish in the new territories. Opponents of slavery argued bitterly against its spread.

On August 8, 1846, Congressman David Wilmot of Pennsylvania had introduced a controversial proposal. He proposed that slavery never "exist in any part" of any land that may be acquired from Mexico. Southerners furiously opposed the "Wilmot Proviso," as it was known. It passed the House of Representatives but was defeated in the Senate.

Senator John C. Calhoun of South Carolina wanted Congress to pass quite a different proposal. He said that neither Congress nor a territorial government should have the power to ban slavery from a territory or regulate slavery in any way. Calhoun's proposal was defeated in the House. Senator Lewis Cass of Michigan had yet another idea. He suggested leaving the question of slavery in the territories up to the people in each territory. Cass's idea, called "popular sovereignty," was not pursued at that time.

"There is no right on the part of any one or more of the States to secede. . . . War and dissolution of the Union are identical and inevitable."

Henry Clay, January 29, 1850

The Compromise of 1850

The question of California came up next. In 1849, Californians adopted a constitution that prohibited slavery. They then asked to be admitted to the Union as a state. California's statehood got tangled up with other issues. One was that antislavery people wanted to ban slavery in the nation's capital, Washington, D.C. Another was that Southerners wanted to strengthen the federal law requiring states to return fugitive, or runaway, slaves to their owners. (At this time, many slaves ran away from the slave states in the South to free states in the North.)

There were now 15 each of slave and free states. If California were admitted as a free state, and New Mexico, Oregon, and Utah followed as free states, the South would be hopelessly outvoted in Congress. Fearing this situation, some Southerners were talking about having their states secede from, or leave, the United States. A terrible crisis was at hand.

In January 1850, a great debate on all these questions began in the U.S. Senate. Pleading to preserve the Union, Henry Clay, now a senator, presented a compromise plan. To settle all the major disputes, he made the following proposals:

- that California be admitted as a free state;
- that territorial governments be formed in the rest of the land acquired from Mexico, but with no mention of slavery one way or the other;
- that the buying and selling of slaves, but not slavery itself, be abolished in Washington, D.C.;
- that a more effective law concerning the return of fugitive slaves be passed and enforced.

Senator Calhoun opposed Clay's plan. He was too ill to

Henry Clay speaks to the Senate in February 1850. Clay was 72 years old when the great debate on slavery began in Congress. He had been influential in other important decisions made by the government, going all the way back to the War of 1812. The Compromise of 1850 earned him the name "The Great Pacificator."

deliver his own speech, so it was read for him by another senator. Calhoun said the only way to save the Union would be to allow Southerners to carry their "property"—their slaves—wherever they wished. If California was admitted as a free state, the Southern states could not "remain in the Union consistently with their honor and safety."

Daniel Webster of Massachusetts replied to Calhoun. He said what was important was to preserve the Union. After many months of bargaining, Congress finally passed a series of laws in September 1850 that closely resembled Clay's plan. Crowds gathered and celebrated that the Union was saved. A convention of Southerners who had talked about seceding disbanded without doing anything. President Millard Fillmore said the 1850 Compromise was a "final settlement" of the conflict between North and South. But he was wrong.

"I wish to speak today, not as a Massachusetts man, nor as a Northern man, but as an American. . . . I speak today for the preservation of the Union. Hear me for my cause."

Daniel Webster, March 7, 1850

Southern Knights and Ladies

Wealthy Southern slaveholders thought of themselves as a special class, claiming incorrectly they were descendants of English nobility. In contrast, they thought, Northerners were the descendants of lower-class Englishmen.

Many prominent Southern men saw themselves as born leaders. They created a code of ideal behavior, based on tales of English knights in medieval days. It emphasized honor, courtesy, and gallantry toward women. Dueling was an appropriate way to settle disputes between gentlemen. One governor of South Carolina reputedly fought 14 duels.

Military values were more highly prized in the South than in the North. Most of the top generals before the Civil War were Southerners. In 1860, there were five times as many military schools in the South as in the North.

A special role was created for Southern women, too. The wealthy planter's wife was idealized as a delicate creature of great beauty, charm, and graciousness. Her place was in the home, and she took no part in public life. Although the reality is now different, images of gallantry, military values, and the southern belle endure in Southern white society in the same way that the West is today still associated with the spirit of pioneers and frontier living.

2

The Road to Civil War

The calm that followed the Compromise of 1850 did not last long. Many Northerners were outraged by the new Fugitive Slave Act. As early as the 1790s, Congress had passed laws to help slaveholders catch slaves who had run away, but the new law provoked more bad feelings than ever before.

This painting by Eastman Johnson, called "A Ride for Liberty," shows fugitive slaves trying to escape to freedom. The Fugitive Slave Act, part of the Compromise of 1850, was a harsh law that helped slave owners recapture escaped slaves.

The Fugitive Slave Act

Under the Fugitive Slave Act, runaway slaves could not testify in their own defense. Anyone who aided the runaway could be fined or imprisoned. Even a person who refused to help in capturing an escaped slave could be punished.

Slaveholders increased their efforts to catch fugitives, even of those slaves who had been living in the North for years. In some cases, free blacks who were not in fact runaways were seized and made slaves. The federal government helped slaveholders catch runaways, sometimes at great expense. Many Northerners refused to help. Mobs prevented, or tried to prevent, the recapture of escaped slaves. Some Northern states passed laws to keep escaped slaves from being sent back to their masters.

Harriet Beecher Stowe (1811–96) and *Uncle Tom's Cabin*

The writer Harriet Beecher Stowe was born in Connecticut. Her father and one of her brothers were prominent ministers and abolitionists. Harriet married a minister, Calvin Stowe, who became a professor of religion. In Cincinnati, where the Stowes lived for 18 years, Stowe encountered many runaway slaves.

Stowe began writing to help support her large family. She strongly opposed the Fugitive Slave Act of 1850, and her feelings inspired her to write the novel *Uncle Tom's Cabin; or, Life Among the Lowly*. Published in 1852, the novel was filled with vivid characters. Stowe wanted to persuade readers of the evil of slavery, and the book shows the problems slavery caused for whites as well as blacks. It became a best-seller and was turned into a popular play.

Uncle Tom's Cabin led many Americans to think more seriously about the slavery problem. Even Southerners rushed to buy the book, although some communities tried to ban it. Despite Stowe's efforts to be fair, reviewers in the South furiously criticized her. Proslavery writers responded to the book by writing novels that claimed slaves lived better lives than free workers in the North.

Bleeding Kansas

In 1854, a new sectional crisis over slavery erupted. Senator Stephen A. Douglas, a Democrat from Illinois, introduced a bill to organize the Louisiana Purchase land west of Iowa and Missouri into the territories of Kansas and Nebraska. According to the Missouri Compromise, Nebraska and Kansas would eventually become free states because they were located north of 36°30' latitude. Douglas's bill proposed to change that. It would allow settlers in each territory to decide about slavery. This was the popular sovereignty principle, first introduced by Senator Cass in 1847.

The proposal reopened the dispute in Congress about slavery in the territories. The North was split over Douglas's plan. Antislavery people bitterly opposed the repeal of the Missouri Compromise. Southerners in Congress, however, backed it unanimously. Thanks to them, the Kansas-Nebraska Act became law in May 1854.

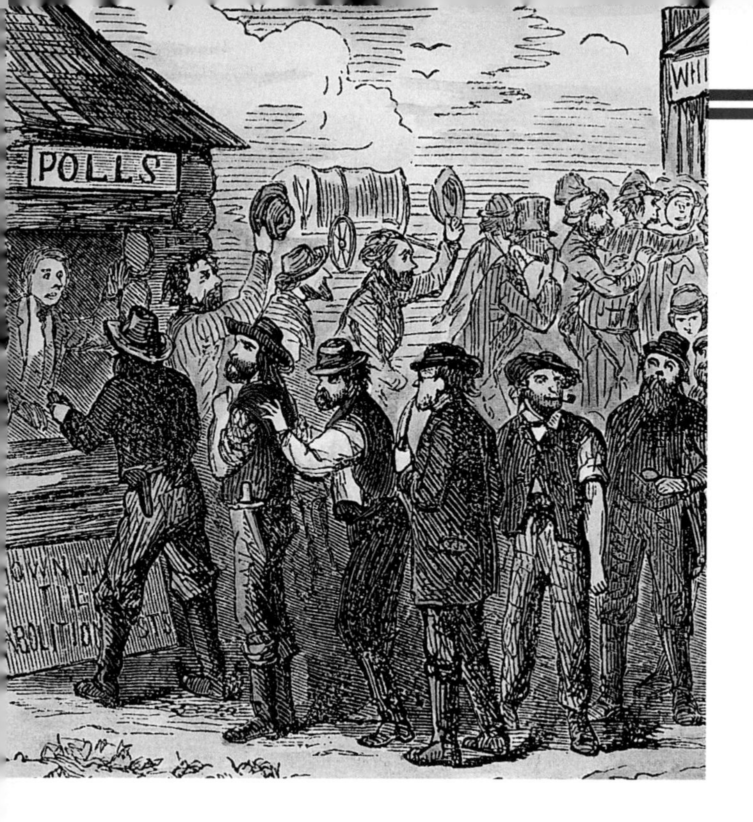

The men who came from Missouri to vote illegally in the Kansas elections of 1855 were known as "border ruffians." Over the next few years, fighting raged between these supporters of slavery and the free-soil activists who wanted Kansas to outlaw slavery.

According to popular sovereignty, voters in a territory would decide whether to permit slavery. That sounded simple, but applying popular sovereignty in Kansas produced a disaster. Both proslavery and antislavery groups rushed to send supporters into Kansas. The proslavery people, many of them armed, got there first. Kansas held elections in spring 1855 for a territorial legislature. Although only about 1,500 voters lived in Kansas then, 6,000 people voted. Proslavery people from Missouri had come in just to vote in the election, and a proslavery legislature was elected.

Antislavery Kansans armed themselves, too. They held their own election and adopted a constitution that banned slavery. Thus, by January 1856, there were two governments in Kansas, one proslavery and one antislavery. Each asked for recognition by Congress.

Then came violence, as both sides committed murders and burnings. For a time, not even the United States Army could stop it. Newspapers began referring to "Bleeding Kansas" and "the Civil War in Kansas." The fighting proved that popular sovereignty could not peacefully solve the disagreement over slavery. (Later, in 1859, fair elections showed that the majority of Kansans wanted their territory to become a free state.)

The Rise of the Republican Party

For the previous 20 years, the Democrats and the Whigs had been America's two main political parties. But now, the agitation over the Fugitive Slave Act and, even more, the Kansas-Nebraska Act, led to the breakup of the Whig party. By the mid-1850s, it had disappeared.

Violence in Congress

As Congress was considering which Kansas government to recognize, Senator Charles Sumner of Massachusetts delivered a fiery two-day speech called "The Crime against Kansas." He criticized proslavery people in extremely vicious language. Sumner was especially harsh on South Carolina's Senator Andrew P. Butler.

Butler was absent at the time. A few days later, his nephew, Congressman Preston Brooks, walked into the Senate chamber, where Sumner was sitting at his desk. Brooks repeatedly beat Sumner over the head and shoulders with a heavy cane. Bleeding heavily, Sumner fell to the floor unconscious. He was so badly injured, both physically and mentally, that it was four years before he could return to the Senate.

To antislavery Northerners, the incident showed how slavery brought evil. But in the South, Brooks became a hero. He resigned from Congress but was unanimously reelected. No proceedings were taken against him, and supporters sent him dozens of new canes. Some were inscribed "Hit Him Again."

Antislavery Whigs, people who had been members of the Free-Soil party, and a few antislavery Democrats held meetings around the country in the spring and summer of 1854. A new political party was being born. The new antislavery party chose candidates who campaigned vigorously in the 1854 state and congressional elections. They called themselves "Republicans."

The Republicans took over the Whig program of high taxes and federal support for economic growth. They also addressed local issues that were important in various parts of the North. But the party's main message was that slavery should not be allowed to spread into new territories. They said that instead these lands should be settled and worked by whites. In the fall elections of 1854, Republicans won more than 100 seats in Congress and gained control of several state legislatures in the North.

"[We must] rally as one man for the establishment of liberty and the overthrow of the Slave Power."

National Era, *May 22, 1854*

James Buchanan was inaugurated as president on March 4, 1857. In his inaugural speech, he declared that, to save the Union, slavery should be tolerated. He said that sectional parties, those that cared only about the interests of their own region, should be destroyed.

The 1856 Presidential Election

The main contenders in the 1856 presidential election were the Republicans and the Democrats. For president, the Republicans nominated the explorer John C. Frémont of California. The Republican slogan was "Free Soil, Free Speech, and Frémont."

The Democratic candidate was James Buchanan of Pennsylvania. Despite what had happened in Kansas, the Democrats supported popular sovereignty. They attacked the Republicans as a sectional party and accused them of being abolitionists. Some Southern Democrats threatened secession if the Republicans won.

Buchanan won the election. He received almost 500,000 more popular votes than Frémont, who got hardly any votes in the South. What was remarkable, however, was that Frémont still received about a third of all the votes cast. He ran very strongly in the North.

The Dred Scott Decision

During Buchanan's term, relations between North and South worsened quickly. Two days after Buchanan took office in 1857, the Supreme Court handed down a decision in a case involving slavery. The decision would have a tremendous impact on the country.

Dred Scott was a slave in Missouri. He had been taken for a while by his owner to Illinois, a free state, and to Wisconsin Territory, where slavery had been banned by the Missouri Compromise. Advised by abolitionist lawyers, Scott claimed in a law suit that he should be a free man because he had lived in free areas. Speaking for the Supreme Court, Chief Justice Roger B. Taney ruled, first, that black people were not citizens, and so Dred Scott could not even start a law suit. Moreover, Scott's residence in free territory did not make him free. A slave was property, and the Constitution prohibits the taking away of a person's property without "due process of law." Furthermore, the Court said, the Missouri Compromise had been unconstitutional. Popular sovereignty was unconstitutional as well. Not even the voters in a territory could ban slavery, since that would be taking away a person's "property."

The Dred Scott decision divided the country more than ever. Proslavery Southerners were overjoyed because the Supreme Court had reaffirmed what they had always maintained: Nothing could legally prevent the spread of slavery. Senator Douglas of Illinois and other Northern Democrats were not happy. The decision had undercut the popular sovereignty idea that they thought could solve the slavery problem. Republicans and other antislavery people were horrified by the decision.

The Debates of 1858

The Dred Scott decision and other aspects of the slavery problem were discussed in a historic series of debates in 1858. Illinois was holding an election for the U.S. Senate and Douglas was running for reelection. Opposing him was a lesser known man, Republican Abraham Lincoln. Lincoln decided to challenge Douglas to a series of debates. The two agreed to seven joint appearances throughout Illinois in the summer and fall. Thousands of people came to hear the debates, standing or sitting outdoors for hours. Newspapers told the rest of the nation what was said.

Each man expressed himself well. Lincoln made clear his opposition to slavery and his hope that eventually it would be ended. Douglas accused Lincoln of working for the breakup of

In 1858, Republican Abraham Lincoln ran for the United States Senate against Democrat Senator Stephen Douglas of Illinois. The two candidates took part in a series of public debates (below). Although Douglas won the election and retained his seat, his opponent won fame and public support.

"A house divided against itself cannot stand. I believe this government cannot endure, permanently half slave and half free."

Abraham Lincoln, the Lincoln-Douglas Debates, 1858

"[If the states] cannot endure thus divided, then [he] must strive to make them all free or all slave, which will inevitably bring about a dissolution of the Union. . . . [People in the territories] have the lawful means to introduce or exclude [slavery] as they please.

Stephen A. Douglas, the Lincoln-Douglas Debates, 1858

the Union. Regardless of the Dred Scott decision, Douglas still thought popular sovereignty the best solution because, he said, slavery needed local laws to protect it. Thus, he argued, if the local citizens didn't support slavery, it couldn't survive. He appealed to the antiblack prejudices of the voters, who were all white. He accused Lincoln of wanting blacks to be fully equal to whites. Lincoln denied this, but said blacks had as much right to earn a free living as whites.

In one sense, Douglas won the debates, as Illinois reelected him to the Senate. However, the debates made Lincoln a nationally known Republican leader. In the North generally, Republicans gained more seats in Congress in the 1858 elections. Southerners were increasingly fearful that the North meant to destroy slavery.

John Brown

In October 1859, an event occurred that fed those fears. John Brown, an abolitionist from Connecticut, passionately hated slavery on religious and moral grounds. During the violence in Kansas, with murders being committed by both sides, Brown had killed five proslavery men in 1856. In October 1859, encouraged and financed by abolitionists, he led a group of whites and blacks in a raid against the United States arsenal at Harper's Ferry, Virginia. (See map on page 32.) Brown hoped to spark an uprising of slaves, whom he would arm with the weapons he seized from the arsenal.

The plan failed. No slaves rebelled, and soldiers quickly captured Brown and his group. Brown was put on trial for treason and found guilty. He and six of his followers were hanged on December 2, 1859. The trial and executions caused a sensation throughout America. Some antislavery people in the North denounced Brown's actions, but to others he was a great hero. Southerners, on the other hand, were horrified by Brown's raid. When his connections to abolitionists became known, Southerners felt this confirmed the existence of a great Northern conspiracy against the South and against slavery.

The Election of 1860

The nation was on the brink of disaster as the 1860 presidential election approached. Tensions between North and South were higher than ever before. In the South, there was more talk of secession.

As Democrats met to choose their presidential candidate, Southern delegates insisted that the party officially support protection for slavery in the United States territories. Douglas and most Northern delegates would not go along. The Northern Democrats chose Douglas for president and endorsed popular sovereignty. Southerners walked out and later held their own meeting. At that meeting, they nominated John C. Breckinridge of Kentucky (who was vice president at the time) for president. The Southern Democrats adopted Calhoun's old position, saying neither Congress nor the territorial legislatures could prevent citizens from settling "with their property," meaning slaves, in any of the territories.

The Republicans nominated Abraham Lincoln for president. They came out squarely against the "legal existence of Slavery in any Territory." A fourth candidate was John Bell of Tennessee. He was nominated by a group from both North and South. Known as the Constitutional Union party, it stressed its devotion to the Constitution and the Union. They took no position on slavery.

The election was hard fought, but with the Democrats divided, Lincoln won a clear victory. He got 189 electoral votes, more than enough for a majority. Lincoln was not

John Brown, seen here on the way to his execution in 1859, has often been called a "fanatic." Convinced by his Christian beliefs that slavery was a moral outrage, Brown was prepared to shed blood and die for his cause. But at the time of his trial and execution, many people were impressed with his sanity and commitment to abolition. The governor of Virginia said, "They are themselves mistaken who take him for a madman."

Abraham Lincoln (1809–65)

Abraham Lincoln was the sixteenth president of the United States. Born in Kentucky in 1809, he and his family moved to Illinois when he was 11. As a youth, Lincoln was very poor and had very little formal education. But he was intelligent and ambitious, and eventually became a prosperous lawyer.

In 1842, Lincoln married Mary Todd, with whom he had four children, all boys. He was a great storyteller and had many friends, yet he was often unhappy. He once said, "If what I felt were equally distributed to the whole human family, there would not be one cheerful face on earth." Lincoln's unquestioned honesty earned him the nickname "Honest Abe."

Lincoln joined the Whig party in the 1830s but was not at first very successful in politics, serving just one term in Congress in the 1840s. After the Kansas-Nebraska debate, he became a Republican. Lincoln thought slavery was morally wrong, although he admitted he did not know what to do about it where it already existed. He was certain, however, it should not be allowed to expand.

Lincoln was elected president in 1860 and reelected in 1864. As president, nearly all his attention was devoted to the Civil War. The war had just ended when Lincoln was shot on April 14, 1865. He died the next day. Millions of people watched the train carrying his coffin as it traveled from Washington back to Illinois.

"We have just carried an election on principles fairly stated to the people. Now we are told . . . the government shall be broken up, unless we surrender to those we have beaten."

Abraham Lincoln, December 10, 1860

even on the ballot in most Southern states, but he won almost all the electoral votes from the other states. His total popular vote, almost 1.9 million, was not a majority but was more than any other candidate's. In effect, the North, with its greater population, had outvoted the South.

The South Secedes

Lincoln and the Republicans had promised not to interfere with slavery where it already existed. Nevertheless, Southern opinion leaders warned that the election of a Republican president would destroy the Union. The South now acted to carry out this threat.

South Carolina voted to secede, or leave the Union, in December 1860. By February 1861, Texas, Louisiana, Mississippi, Alabama, Florida, and Georgia had done the same. At this time, Virginia, North Carolina, Tennessee, and Arkansas chose not to leave the Union. They announced they would secede, however, if the United States used force against the South.

Jefferson Davis (1808–89)

Jefferson Davis, the only president of the Confederate States of America, was born in Kentucky. His family soon moved to Mississippi, where they owned a large plantation.

Davis graduated from West Point Military Academy in 1828 and fought in frontier wars against Native Americans. He married Sarah Knox, daughter of Zachary Taylor (who later became president) in 1835. She died after only three months of marriage, and in 1845 Davis married Varina Howell, with whom he had six children.

Davis entered the House of Representatives as a Democrat from Mississippi in 1845. The next year, however, he resigned to fight in the Mexican War. He later became a U.S. senator and was secretary of war under President Franklin Pierce. He was again a senator when Mississippi seceded from the Union early in 1861.

As president of the Confederacy, Davis worked very hard. But he failed to inspire people and mistakenly thought he had great military talent. When the Confederacy collapsed, Davis fled southward to Georgia, where he was captured. He was imprisoned and accused of treason, although he was never tried and was released in 1867. In 1881, Davis published a history entitled *The Rise and Fall of the Confederate Government.*

"... the constitutional compact has been deliberately broken and disregarded by the non-slaveholding States; and the consequence follows that South Carolina is released from her obligation."

South Carolina, "Declaration of the Causes of Secession," December 20, 1860

"All hope of relief in the Union ... is extinguished, and we trust the South will not be deceived by appearances or the pretence of new guarantees. ... The honor, safety, and independence of the Southern people are to be found only in a Southern Confederacy."

Address to Constituents by 30 Southern Congressmen, December 13, 1860

Delegates from the seven seceding states met in Montgomery, Alabama, to form a new nation and government. They used the theory of states' rights to justify leaving the Union. They said the states had voluntarily chosen to enter the Union in 1789. But the government of the Union had violated the rights of the states, and so they were justified in seceding. They called themselves the "Confederate States of America," or "the Confederacy." Jefferson Davis, just elected a senator from Mississippi, was chosen as president of the Confederacy.

The Crisis Deepens

Many Southerners were delighted. In Charleston, South Carolina, for example, church bells rang, cannons were fired, and people celebrated in the streets. Others worried about the future. In the North, some abolitionists felt that if the Union could be maintained only by compromising with slavery, then it was better to let it be destroyed. Most Northerners and President-elect Lincoln, however, rejected that idea. They thought the Union must be preserved.

For those determined to save the Union, the question was, how can it be done? Lincoln had been elected president, but President Buchanan was still in office. His term ran until March 4, 1861. In his last message to Congress, Buchanan said states did not have the right to secede. But he went on to say that he had no power to stop them. Lincoln disagreed. To him, it was the president's duty to enforce the laws and preserve the existing government. The seceding states were breaking the law. If they used force, they would be committing treason, and treason must be put down.

In Washington, some leaders worked frantically to find a last-minute compromise that would save the Union. Senator John J. Crittenden of Kentucky proposed amendments to the Constitution, including a plan to protect slavery south of the old Missouri Compromise line. To Republicans, this was unacceptable, and leaders of the seceding states also rejected the idea. There appeared to be no solution.

Fort Sumter

In his Inaugural Address, President Lincoln said secession would not be permitted. However, he faced terribly difficult decisions. Confederate forces had already seized some United States forts, and Lincoln did not want to start a war by trying to take them back.

On March 5, 1861, the day after he was inaugurated, Lincoln read a dispatch from the commander of Fort Sumter, a U.S. post on an island in Charleston Harbor, off South Carolina. (See map on page 32.) The fort was running out of food, and Confederates had already fired on a ship that was attempting to deliver supplies to it. Lincoln sent a message to the Confederates. He said he was ordering an unarmed expedition with supplies to Fort Sumter, and that Union forces would not fire unless fired upon. In this way, Lincoln left the decision to start the shooting up to the Confederates.

On April 11, Confederate officers arrived at the fort and demanded its immediate surrender. The fort's commander, Major Robert Anderson, refused, and the Confederate guns

"We are not enemies, but friends. We must not be enemies. Though passion may have strained, it must not break our bonds of affection."

Abraham Lincoln, on preserving the Union in his First Inaugural Address, March 4, 1861

In the attack on Fort Sumter, the Confederates fired more than 3,000 shells. Fires were soon blazing all over the fort.

opened fire on Fort Sumter on April 12. After a two-day bombardment, in which no one was killed, the fort at last surrendered.

On April 15, President Lincoln issued a call for 75,000 volunteers to fight to save the Union. The Civil War had begun. Over the next six weeks, Virginia, North Carolina, Tennessee, and Arkansas joined the Confederacy. In May 1861, after Virginia seceded, the Confederate capital was moved from Montgomery, Alabama, to Richmond, Virginia, only about 100 miles (160 km) from Washington, D.C., the capital of the United States.

Political Campaigns and Debates

After political parties emerged in the 1790s, political campaigning came into being as parties tried to persuade people to vote for their candidates. Before the days of radio and television, campaigning was a simpler process. Speaking in public about their policies was the politicians' main tool, and meetings to support candidates were held in towns all over the nation. Newspaper reports of campaign speeches were a vital part of the process, as many people would have to vote without ever seeing or hearing the candidate they chose.

Public debates between political opponents became an important part of election campaigns. During the historic debates of 1858, Lincoln and Douglas spoke for many hours at a time directly to crowds of listeners. They had no microphones or loudspeakers to amplify their voices. Today's political debates are somewhat different. Reporters ask questions, and the candidates have only a few minutes to reply. While an audience may be present, many more people watch the debates on television. Within minutes of the end of the debate, public opinion polls tell us which candidate "won" the debate.

Today, television has become the main factor in the success of political campaigns. Millions of dollars are spent on creating an attractive image of the candidates. How well they and their policies are presented on television can sometimes seem more important than the policies themselves.

3

The Early Years of the War

By May 1861, 11 Southern states had seceded to form the Confederate States of America (also called "The Confederacy" or "the South"). The other 22 states remained in the Union (also called "the United States" or "the North").

Choosing Sides

Four states in the Union—Kentucky, Delaware, Maryland, and Missouri—were considering what to do. These states were known as the "border states," and each had significant numbers of slaves in its population. If these border states joined the Confederacy, the Union would be seriously weakened. Maryland was particularly crucial to the Union. If it joined the Confederacy, the capital of the United States would be surrounded.

Fortunately for the North, all four states stayed in the Union. The situation caused serious problems for President Lincoln, however. There were strong pro-Confederacy groups in Missouri, Kentucky, and Maryland, and feeling against slavery was weak in all three states. So Lincoln had to be very cautious. If he made ending slavery a goal of the war, the groups sympathetic to the Confederacy might gain control of the border states and take them out of the Union.

Sometimes, however, Lincoln had to act boldly. Early in the war, Confederate sympathizers in Maryland attacked Union soldiers, destroyed telegraph lines to Washington, and burned railroad bridges. Lincoln sent troops to the state and arrested the pro-Confederate leaders. For a time, he even

"Our new government is founded . . . upon the great truth that the negro is not equal to the white man; that slavery—subordination to the superior race—is his natural and normal condition."

Alexander H. Stephens, vice president of the Confederacy, March 21, 1861

This map shows why the border states were important to the Union. Missouri, along the Mississippi River, controlled the major routes to the West. Kentucky controlled another key river, the Ohio. Delaware was small, but it could threaten the major city of Philadelphia, Pennsylvania. Maryland's loss would be a disaster: Important railroad lines passed through it, and it bordered Washington, D.C., on three sides. The fourth side of the city faced Virginia across the Potomac River.

took away some constitutional rights from Maryland citizens accused of crimes.

Within the Confederacy, too, some states were divided. Tennessee and Alabama had significant pro-Union groups in some areas, as did Virginia. In northwestern Virginia, a movement formed to secede from the state and rejoin the Union. Forty-eight counties organized themselves as a separate state called West Virginia, and Congress admitted this new state to the Union in 1863.

The Two Sides

As the two sides prepared for war, the North did appear to have clear advantages over the South. Both its population and its economy were far larger. The North had many more of the resources needed to wage war. It had a better banking system to raise the money needed to pay for war; and it had many more ships.

The Confederacy was based on the idea of states' rights, which meant its leaders did not believe in a strong central government. This weakened its war effort because Southern states were reluctant to give the Confederate government enough power to fight the war effectively.

Yet the South had some important advantages, especially at the start of the war. Southerners were fighting on their own soil, in defense of their homes, and were more united behind their cause than Northerners were. In addition, their military leadership was, at first, superior to that of the North. The South also expected help from abroad. Britain and France needed the cotton the South exported, and Confederate leaders thought these nations would help them establish independence.

The two sides had different aims. President Lincoln made it clear from the start that the goal of the North was to bring all the Southern states back into the Union. The North never officially recognized the Confederacy as a separate nation. The seceding Southerners were considered rebels who had broken the law. At the beginning of the war, ending slavery was not the North's goal. This would change as the war went on, however.

For the Confederate States, the aim of the war was to win recognition as an independent nation. In this way, the South thought, it could preserve its traditional way of life. That way of life, of course, included slavery.

Free States and Slave States

The United States could be divided into those states that allowed slavery and those that did not. The 11 Southern states that seceded to form the Confederacy were all slave states. The border states listed below also officially permitted slavery, but chose to side with the North, or free states, when war broke out in 1861.

The Union (Free States)
California, Connecticut, Illinois, Indiana, Iowa, Maine, Massachusetts, Michigan, Minnesota, New Hampshire, New Jersey, New York, Ohio, Oregon, Pennsylvania, Rhode Island, Vermont, Wisconsin

The Union (Slave, or Border States)
Delaware, Kentucky, Maryland, Missouri

The Confederacy (Slave States)
Alabama, Arkansas, Florida, Georgia, Louisiana, Mississippi, North Carolina, South Carolina, Tennessee, Texas, Virginia

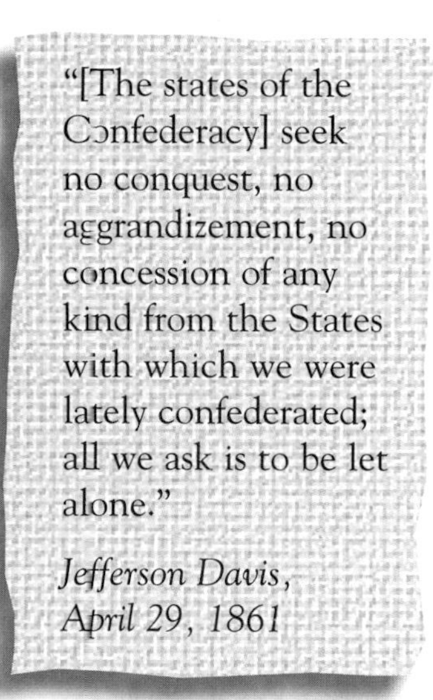

"[The states of the Confederacy] seek no conquest, no aggrandizement, no concession of any kind from the States with which we were lately confederated; all we ask is to be let alone."

Jefferson Davis, April 29, 1861

Strategies in the North and the South

At the start of the war, the Union's strategy for winning was to do three things. First, using its superior navy, the North would blockade, or close, Southern ports. This would stop essential supplies from coming into the South and prevent it from selling its main product, cotton. Second, the Union intended to gain control of the Mississippi and Tennessee Rivers. This would split Confederate territory and also help prevent supplies coming up from the Gulf of Mexico. Finally, the North wanted to capture Richmond, the capital of the Confederate States of America.

The South's plan was to hold out until the North got tired of fighting and agreed to recognize the independence of the Confederacy. When the opportunity arose, however, Southern armies would move north and perhaps capture or at least threaten Washington, D.C., and other Northern cities. The South also expected that Britain's and France's need for Southern cotton would cause them to pressure the North to give up the fight. Until that happened, the South would sell its cotton to those countries for the guns and other materials it needed. Eventually, Southerners hoped, the North would see that it could not win the war.

The First Battle

By the summer of 1861, the Confederate Army had a total of about 112,000 men, known as the "Rebels." The total number of Union soldiers, or "Yankees," was about 187,000.

These Union ships at anchor in the James River, Virginia, in 1864 formed part of the blockades that were so important to Union strategy. By the middle of the war, the blockades had reduced Southern trade by two-thirds. Goods like coffee, shoes, cloth, nails, and salt—as well as guns and ammunition—were in short supply.

Over the course of the entire war, about 900,000 men served in the Confederate Army, and more than 2 million in the Union Army. On both sides, most of the soldiers were very young and inexperienced. Many were just teenagers.

Sunday, July 21, 1861, was a hot, sunny day. Parties of Washington residents drove out of the city and across the Potomac River to have a picnic in Virginia. They were going to watch the first major battle of the Civil War. Expecting to see the Union Army crush the Confederates, they looked forward to an enjoyable day. For their part, the Confederates also anticipated an easy victory and a short war.

This first battle was fought in northern Virginia, at a place called Manassas Junction near Bull Run Creek. The battle is usually called the First Battle of Bull Run. About 30,000 inexperienced Union troops under General Irwin McDowell attacked an equally inexperienced Confederate force of about the same size under General Pierre Beauregard.

The First Battle of Bull Run in Virginia was a victory for the Confederates, but it was also a bloody fight in which about 870 soldiers were killed. The two armies buried their dead along the Bull Run, the stream by which the battle took place. The Union soldiers in the foreground below belonged to the Zouaves, an army unit that copied its brightly-colored uniform and some of its military routines from the French-Algerian infantry unit of the same name.

"This Union your ancestors and mine helped to make must be saved from destruction."

Ted Upson, 16-year-old Union soldier from Indiana

"[William is] wild to be off to Virginia. He so fears that the fighting will be over before he can get there."

Kate Stone, sister of William Stone, Confederate soldier from Louisiana

Crying "On to Richmond!" the Yankees at first drove the Confederates back. But the Rebels rallied, inspired by a brigade led by Thomas J. Jackson. Jackson was observed holding out "like a stone wall," which earned him his nickname of "Stonewall" Jackson. The Confederates then counterattacked, and the Union lines broke. Many soldiers panicked and fled back to Washington. They had to push aside the civilians who had come to watch. Although the Confederates had won the battle, they were too disorganized and weakened themselves to pursue the retreating Yankees. Nevertheless, Southerners rejoiced.

In the North, people were shocked. Slowly, the understanding grew that the war would be a long, hard, and costly struggle. President Lincoln was depressed but determined. Throughout the North, men crowded into army recruiting offices to volunteer to fight. For several months, both sides built up their strength.

Battles in Tennessee and Mississippi

The North pursued its strategy to gain control of the Mississippi and Tennessee Rivers and thereby split the South in two. In February 1862, Union forces under General

Americans Fight Americans

The Civil War was not only a war between North and South. In some cases, it was a war within families. This happened most often in the border states. President Lincoln's wife, Mary, was from Kentucky. She had a brother and three half brothers who were in the Confederate Army. In a few instances, family members actually fought each other. In one battle, a Union regiment from West Virginia attacked a Confederate regiment from Virginia. The commanders of the two opposing regiments were cousins.

The great poet Walt Whitman served as a hospital volunteer during the Civil War. He told of two wounded Maryland brothers unknowingly lying in the same hospital. They were on opposite sides in the war and had not seen each other since the war began. They both died.

Ulysses S. Grant captured Forts Henry and Donelson in northern Tennessee. These victories helped keep neighboring Kentucky in the Union. Pro-Confederates there had been trying to persuade the state to secede.

Grant then headed south toward Corinth, Mississippi, an important railroad junction. His army had about 40,000 men. On the morning of April 6, 1862, the Yankees were at Shiloh, Tennessee, just north of Corinth. There, they were suddenly attacked by a Confederate force of the same size. The battle lasted two days. On the first day, one of the Rebel commanders, Albert Sidney Johnston, was killed. Union General William Tecumseh Sherman was wounded twice. On the second day, aided by 25,000 reinforcements, the Yankees drove the Rebels off.

The cost of the battle was terrible. The Union suffered 13,000 killed and wounded; the Confederates almost 11,000. In total, that was more than all the losses of the American Revolution, the War of 1812, and the Mexican War combined. There were two main reasons for the heavy losses. First, the armies were much larger than in earlier wars. Second, the rifles, cannons, and other weapons used were more accurate and powerful than they had been previously.

General Ulysses S. Grant (far left, on horseback) leads his men at the Battle of Fort Donelson, Tennessee, in February 1862. The capture of the fort earned Grant a promotion from Brigadier General to Major General.

Union forces took Corinth and went on two months later to take Memphis, Tennessee. They seemed well on their way to gaining control of the Mississippi River. Also in April 1862, Union naval forces under Admiral David G. Farragut captured New Orleans, the largest city in the South. The capture of New Orleans, near the mouth of the Mississippi, meant the Confederacy could no longer use the river to get its goods to sea. In October, Union forces at Perryville turned back a Confederate invasion of Kentucky.

Sea Battles and Blockades

The main naval effort made by the Union during the Civil War was the blockade of Southern ports. A successful blockade would make it difficult for the South to export its cotton and import the supplies necessary to continue the war.

At first, the North did not have enough ships to cover all the ports along the South's coastline, which was 3,500 miles (5,600 km) long. As a result, many Southern ships could sail in and out. Eventually, as the North built more ships, the blockade became more effective. Using both ships and soldiers, the Union gradually captured all the major ports of the Confederacy. The results were significant. As early as July 1861, South Carolinian Mary Chesnut, whose husband was on Confederate President Jefferson Davis's staff, noted in her diary that the blockade was "beginning to shut out" ammunition. Everyday supplies and food also became harder to obtain.

A Confederate attempt to break the Union's blockade led to a historic naval battle in March 1862. At that time, nearly all ships were made of wood. Southerners took over an abandoned Union warship, the *Merrimac*, in the harbor of Norfolk, Virginia, and covered it with iron plates. The refitted ship, renamed the *Virginia*, then attacked a group of Union ships just outside the harbor. The wooden ships were helpless against this new kind of warship, called an "ironclad."

Northern leaders were very alarmed. This one ship could destroy much of the Union Navy and perhaps bombard

Washington, D.C., as well. However, just at that time, the North had built an ironclad of its own in New York Harbor. The *Monitor* was a true ironclad, built entirely of metal, rather than a refitted wooden ship. Described as looking like a "tin can on a shingle," the *Monitor* rushed down to Norfolk. It engaged the *Virginia* in battle on March 9, 1862. This was the first battle in history between ships made of metal. Technically, the battle was a draw as neither ship could sink the other. But the North could build many more ironclads than the South, and so the Northern blockade remained.

The "Battle of the Mighty Ironclads" in March 1862 lasted for five hours, but ended without victory on either side. The Monitor *was like a metal raft with a revolving turret from which its cannon fired. The* Virginia, *or* Merrimac, *was a wooden ship covered in iron plates. Fire from neither vessel could penetrate the other's armor.*

The Seven Days Battles

On land, in Virginia, the North was not doing so well. After the Union defeat at Bull Run, Lincoln had appointed General George B. McClellan to lead the new Army of the Potomac. McClellan spent many months training the army into an effective fighting force. He devised a plan to capture Richmond. Instead of advancing directly overland, General McClellan moved his army by ship to a position southeast of the city. From there, in May 1862, he slowly started to advance toward the Confederate capital.

McClellan was an excellent trainer of soldiers, but faced with the prospect of an actual battle, he never felt his men were ready. He also tended to overestimate the strength of the opposing army. So McClellan inched cautiously toward Richmond. He had nearly 100,000 men ready for battle. The army got so close that the men could hear the city's church bells ringing. Defending the city was the smaller Confederate Army of Northern Virginia, led by Robert E. Lee. Lee was aided by a remarkable cavalry leader, James E. B. "Jeb" Stuart.

In the Seven Days Battles, fought at the end of June 1862, the Confederates attacked the Yankees for six days. The Union troops fought back and killed many of their opponents as they retreated from the attacks. The Rebels eventually drove the Union Army back on the seventh day, July 2, but could not destroy it. Both sides lost many men: About 1,700 Union soldiers were killed, and nearly 3,500 Confederates died.

From the First Battle of Bull Run in 1861 to the terrible bloodshed of Antietam in 1862, the battles of the Civil War raged through the South and into the border state of Maryland.

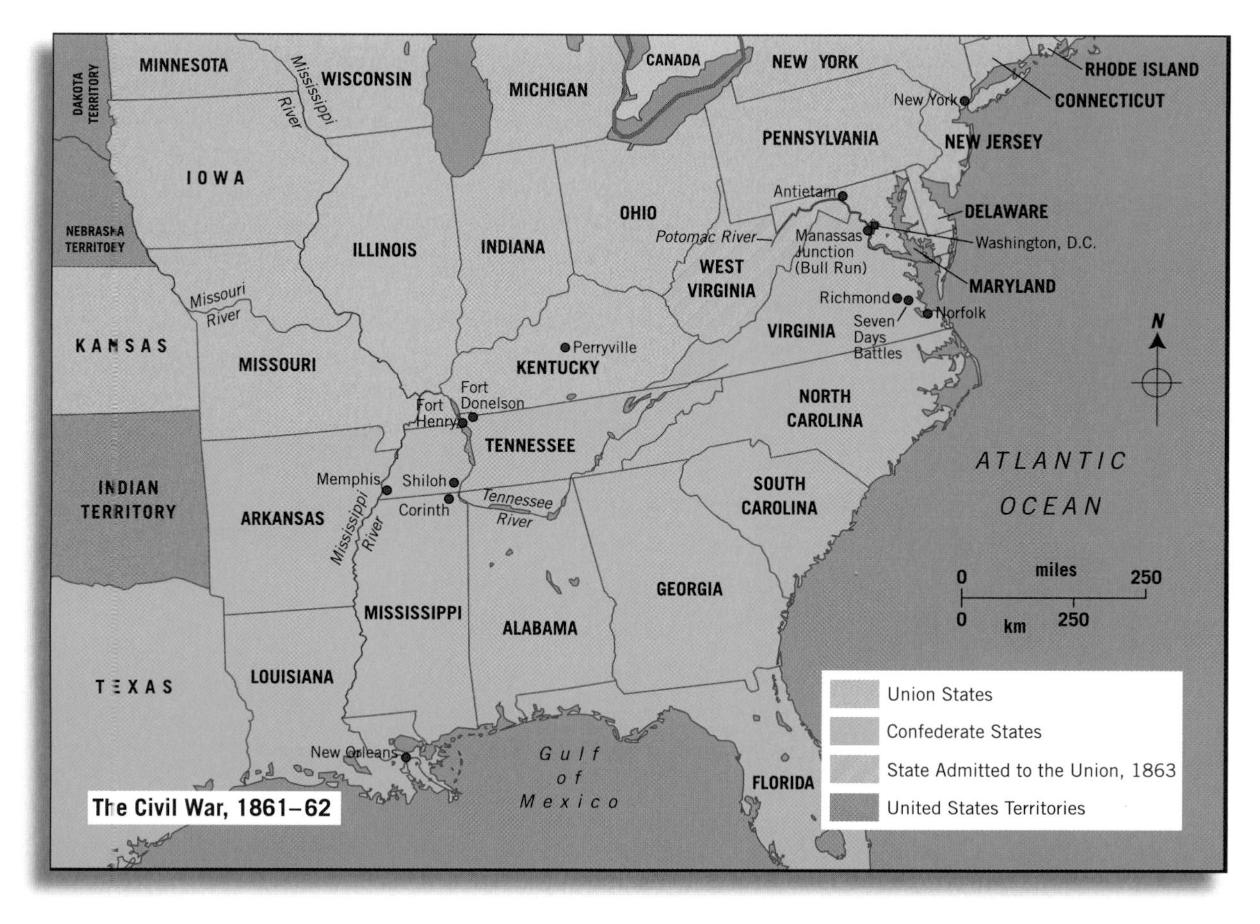

Confederate Generals

Early in the war, the Confederate generals were often superior to their Union opponents. Three of the most famous Confederate generals, all Virginians and all graduates of West Point Military Academy, were Robert E. Lee, Stonewall Jackson, and Jeb Stuart.

Robert E. Lee (1807–70) was one of the greatest generals in American history. The son of a Revolutionary War general, he served with distinction in the Mexican War and was the superintendent of West Point from 1852 to 1855. Lee led the U.S. troops that captured John Brown in 1859. Lee disliked slavery and initially opposed the secession of the Southern states. Early in 1861, President Lincoln offered Lee command of the Union armies. But Lee turned the offer down, feeling he had to be loyal to Virginia. His leadership of the Army of Northern Virginia during the Civil War has been admired by military experts ever since, and he is still famous for his courage and humanity.

Thomas J. "Stonewall" Jackson (1824–63) also fought in the Mexican War and later taught at the Virginia Military Institute. Jackson was a deeply religious man and a fierce believer in the Southern cause. During the Civil War, he conducted a military campaign in Virginia's Shenandoah Valley in 1862 that is still studied for its brilliance. He went on to help the Confederates win the battles of Fredericksburg in 1862 and Chancellorsville in 1863. But at Chancellorsville, he was accidentally shot by his own men. Following the amputation of his arm, Jackson became sick with pneumonia and died.

James E. B. "Jeb" Stuart (1833–64) was Lee's cavalry commander. He fought in Indian wars and assisted Lee in the capture of John Brown. During the Civil War, Stuart served as the "eyes" of Lee's army. He led daring operations that rode around Union positions to gain information. During the Seven Days Battles, Stuart led 1,200 men in a complete circle around the Army of the Potomac to gain valuable information about its positions. Stuart was a dashing character who wore colorful uniforms and a hat with a yellow plume. He was fatally wounded in fighting near Richmond, Virginia, in May 1864.

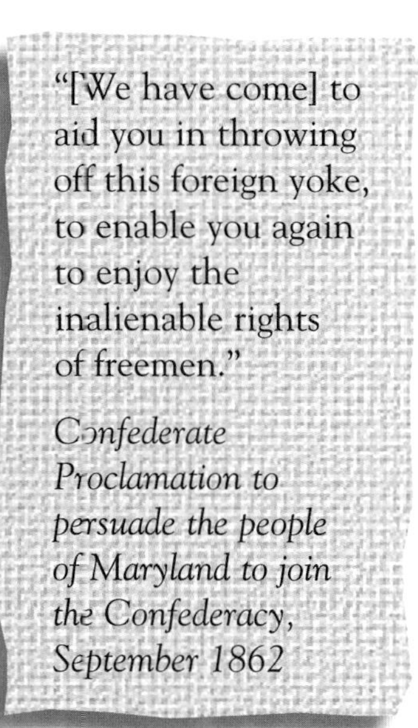

"[We have come] to aid you in throwing off this foreign yoke, to enable you again to enjoy the inalienable rights of freemen."

Confederate Proclamation to persuade the people of Maryland to join the Confederacy, September 1862

Antietam

The Union forces were still strong, and they were only 25 miles (40 km) from Richmond. But McClellan failed to renew the attack. Exasperated, Lincoln ordered him to take the army back to northern Virginia. There, it would join a small force that had remained near Washington, D.C. But before the bulk of McClellan's army could get back, Lee rushed north to battle the Union forces under John Pope. On August 29, 1862, Pope attacked at the Second Battle of Bull Run but was driven back.

Lee, only 20 miles (32 km) away, could now threaten Washington. However, rather than attack Washington directly, Lee moved into Maryland, 40 miles (64 km) north of the city, with 55,000 men. The Confederates hoped to persuade Maryland to join them and to destroy important rail lines in Pennsylvania. They issued a proclamation urging the people of Maryland to join the Confederacy, but it received no response.

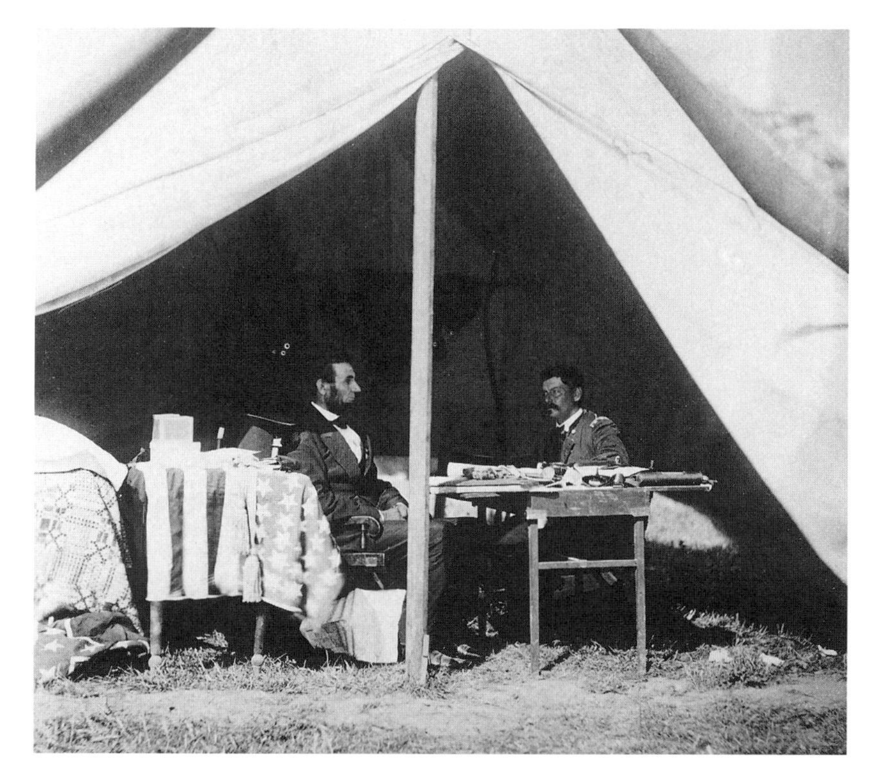

After the Battle of Antietam, President Lincoln (left) went in person to see General McClellan (right) at his Sharpsburg headquarters, near the Antietam battlefields. Lincoln wanted the general to pursue the Confederates into Virginia, but it was more than a month before McClellan finally moved his army, in November 1862. By that time, Lincoln had grown impatient, and he replaced McClellan with General Ambrose Burnside.

McClellan, with 80,000 men, moved slowly after Lee. On September 13, he had an extraordinary piece of good luck. Union soldiers found in a field a copy of Lee's orders to his army. Now McClellan knew the Confederate plans.

The two armies met at Antietam Creek, Maryland, on September 17, 1862. It was the bloodiest single day of the entire war. Each army lost more than 11,000 men. Both armies were badly hurt, but neither was destroyed. The next day, Lee decided to pull back what was left of his army. McClellan had been ordered by Lincoln to "destroy the rebel army." But he failed to pursue Lee.

Lincoln was bitterly disappointed. A few months later, he removed McClellan from command of the Army of the Potomac. Lee's retreat from Antietam, however, had great significance. It enabled Lincoln to do something of immense importance about slavery.

"He has got the slows."

President Lincoln on General McClellan, November 1862

Spies

Governments and armies often use spies to learn things about their enemies. They seek information that can give them an advantage, such as their enemies' plans or the positions of their forces. This was true in the United States' first war, the American Revolution. Nathan Hale of Connecticut was a spy working for George Washington's Continental Army. He was hanged by the British after they captured him on Long Island, New York, in September 1776.

During the Civil War, both North and South employed spies. One Confederate spy was Rose O'Neal Greenhow. She lived in Washington and socialized with important Northern officials. Information she gathered about Yankee plans helped the Confederates win the First Battle of Bull Run in July 1861. In the South, slaves sometimes spied on Confederates to help the North. General McClellan also used a detective agency headed by Allan Pinkerton to gain information about Confederate movements.

Spying is not confined to wartime. Today, the U.S. government uses the Central Intelligence Agency and other organizations to collect information, sometimes through spying, about foreign countries.

4

America During the War

The Civil War profoundly affected the people of America. In both North and South—for soldiers and civilians, whites and blacks, men and women—life changed.

"If I could save the Union without freeing any slave I would do it; and if I could save it by freeing all the slaves I would do it; and if I could save it by freeing some and leaving others alone, I would also do that. . . . I have here stated my purpose according to my view of official duty, and I intend no modification of my oft-expressed personal wish that all men, everywhere could be free."

Abraham Lincoln, August 1862

The Issues Facing Lincoln

In 1861, at the start of the Civil War, few people in the North thought the slaves in the Southern states should be freed. Contrary to what many Southerners believed, abolitionists were only a minority in the North. Lincoln and other Republican leaders had said many times that they were actively opposed only to the expansion of slavery into new areas.

The North's goal in the war was to restore the Union as it had been. President Lincoln made it very clear that he believed this was his primary duty as president. However, his personal feelings were that slaves should be freed.

Slavery existed in the border states, and Lincoln was very concerned about keeping these loyal states in the Union. He knew that there, and in the other Union states as well, making an issue of slavery would divide the people and make the war less popular. As the war went on, however, attitudes began to change. Northerners saw slavery as a help to the Confederate war effort, since every slave who worked enabled a white man to fight in the Confederate Army. So, anything that weakened slavery would be a blow against the South. Congress took the first step by passing laws that declared some slaves free, but only those owned by people active in rebellion against the Union. Next, in 1862, Congress abolished slavery in the District of Columbia.

The great suffering caused by the war contributed to changing attitudes. The ever-increasing number of dead and wounded soldiers seemed to demand a great moral goal that would justify all the suffering. Because of this, ending the moral evil of slavery became for many Northerners a worthy war aim. Lincoln was keenly aware of these shifts in people's feelings. He also knew that striking a blow at slavery would help the Union abroad, as it would make Britain and France less likely to aid the South. This was because both countries were against slavery, so it would be hard for them to take sides with a confederacy fighting for slavery and against a nation that declared its slaves should become free. Most of all, Lincoln was convinced that slavery was helping the South keep on fighting.

Emancipation

By the summer of 1862, Lincoln had decided to declare an end to slavery in the South. This was called "emancipation." Lincoln waited for a suitable moment. He did not want to appear to be acting in desperation when the North seemed to be losing on the battlefield in Virginia. But after Lee's army was turned back at Antietam in September 1862, Lincoln

Lincoln (standing, center) reads the Preliminary Emancipation Proclamation to members of the government. The proclamation, issued on September 22, 1862, said that unless the Confederate states returned to the Union by the new year, their slaves would be freed.

> "We shout for joy that we live to record this righteous decree."
>
> *Frederick Douglass, October 1862*

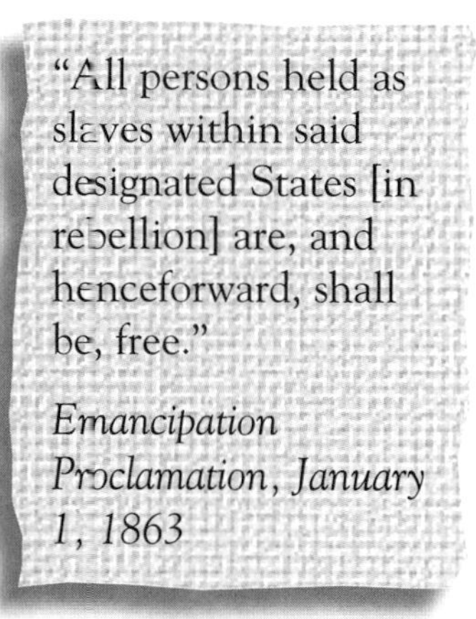

acted. Later in September, he issued the Emancipation Proclamation. It declared all the slaves in areas controlled by the Confederacy to be free as of January 1863. Blacks in the North joyfully greeted the Proclamation. On January 1, 1863, a crowd of black people gathered at the White House to cheer the president.

The Emancipation Proclamation, of course, applied to areas not under Union rule. For that reason, it did not actually free any slaves. But now, Lincoln had put the U.S. government squarely in favor of ending slavery. Moreover, Lincoln knew that many slaves would hear about the Proclamation. He hoped that they would escape from their owners. That is, in fact, what happened. As Union armies approached in the South, thousands of slaves left their owners and moved behind Union lines.

In 1864, Congress prepared a constitutional amendment to abolish slavery everywhere in the United States. Congress passed the amendment in 1865, and it was quickly ratified by loyal states as the Thirteenth Amendment.

Blacks in the South

Both in the South and the North, the war changed the lives of black people. When the war began, there were about 3.5 million slaves in the Confederacy. They made up almost 40 percent of the total Southern population and were vital to the workforce. Many nurses in military hospitals and cooks and drivers in the army were also slaves.

By the end of the war, about a quarter of the Southern slaves were in areas controlled by Union armies. Many of those who remained on their owners' property did not work as hard as before. White Southerners were terrified by the possibility of a slave rebellion. Most were very unwilling to consider using slaves as soldiers because they would have to give the slaves weapons. At the very end of the war, however, the Confederacy was desperate for soldiers. General Lee and President Davis both favored using blacks as soldiers, and said slaves who fought should be freed. The Confederate government then narrowly approved using black soldiers, but very few, if any, blacks actually fought for the Confederacy.

Blacks in the North

At the start of the war, Northern blacks were not permitted to serve as soldiers either. The slaves who escaped behind Union lines also posed a problem. What should be done with them? At first, some Union generals even returned the blacks to their Southern owners. In other cases, blacks were given work helping the Union armies, and those who wished to aid the North found ways to do so. The Navy did accept blacks from the beginning of the war. Southern blacks were especially useful as guides and spies. Harriet Tubman, a former slave, often spied for the North behind Confederate lines.

By 1862, Union leaders needed more soldiers and began to approve the enlistment of black troops. Both free blacks and escaped slaves were allowed to join the Union armies. The Emancipation Proclamation then led to an increase in the number of blacks in the Northern military. By the end of the war, about one of every eight Union soldiers was a black man. All told, more than 180,000 blacks served as soldiers and more than 38,000 died in the fighting. Black soldiers received lower pay than whites at first. After they protested, the pay rates were made equal.

The black soldiers were organized in regiments separate from the rest of the army. Most of their commanding officers were white. One of the most famous black regiments was the 54th Massachusetts. It was commanded by Colonel Robert Gould Shaw, a white. The 54th led the attack of July 18, 1863, on Confederate

In the Civil War, as in Southern life in general, black people were the backbone of the Southern workforce. Although they were not allowed to become soldiers, these slaves helped the Confederate cause by building army fortifications in Georgia.

These members of an honor guard of black Union troops were photographed at Port Hudson, Louisiana. African American soldiers fought bravely for the North, but they were segregated from white soldiers who were reluctant to fight alongside them.

troops near Charleston Harbor, South Carolina. Shaw and nearly half the regiment died in the attack, and their bravery greatly impressed the nation. Altogether, 23 black soldiers won the Medal of Honor during the Civil War.

The Confederates were outraged by the North's use of black soldiers. They threatened to execute any black soldiers they captured. In a few instances, they carried out the threat. In 1864, at Fort Pillow, Tennessee, 262 black soldiers were killed after they had surrendered to the Rebels. Fortunately, such terrible actions were rare.

"O it was too shocking too horrible. God grant that I may never be the partaker in such scenes again. . . . When released from this I shall ever be an advocate of peace."

A Confederate soldier after the Battle of Shiloh, April 1862

The Experience of War

At the start of the war, the mostly young, inexperienced soldiers on both sides did not really know what horrors lay in store for them. When soldiers were wounded, they often received inadequate treatment. During many battles, both sides' medical facilities were overwhelmed. At the Battle of Shiloh in 1862, the wounded lay out in the rain for 24 hours.

Many men deserted. Estimates are that one of every seven Union and one of every nine Confederate soldiers ran away because of fear, hunger, or sickness. Disease and infection killed many more men than bullets did.

This Texas boy enlisted in the Confederate Army, was captured, and died in a northern prison camp at 16.

The Draft

When the war began, men rushed to volunteer for both the Confederate and Union armies. In the South, in fact, so many volunteered that thousands had to be turned away because there was not enough equipment for them. As the war dragged on, however, the number of volunteers declined. Both sides had to resort to new measures to get the manpower they needed.

The Confederate government passed a law in April 1862 that required men between the ages

Fighting for Liberty—Soldiers' Letters from the Civil War

Both Yankee and Rebel soldiers wrote letters home to their loved ones. They told their wives, parents, sisters, and brothers what they were experiencing. Some soldiers died shortly after writing, but many thousands of these letters have survived. From them, we can learn about the ideals the men took with them into the war.

On both sides, soldiers felt they were fighting for liberty. A Virginia officer wrote his mother that the Confederacy's struggle was a "second War of American Independence." The South would win because "tyranny" cannot defeat "a people fighting for their liberties." It seems strange today, but these young Southerners sincerely thought the right to own slaves was an important part of their own freedom. They believed the North was trying to enslave the South. A South Carolinian captain wrote his wife, "Sooner than submit to Northern slavery, I prefer death."

Union soldiers believed the future of freedom depended on them. "I do feel that the liberty of the world is placed in our hands to defend," wrote home a Massachusetts private. A Connecticut soldier said much the same: If "traitors be allowed to overthrow and break asunder ties most sacred—costing our forefathers long years of blood and toil," then "all the hope and confidence of the world in the capacity of men for self-government will be lost."

An event on First Avenue in New York City during the Draft Riots of July 1863. The riots lasted for four violent days. Black people and their homes were attacked, and white citizens opposed to the draft fought in the streets with soldiers.

of 18 and 35 to serve in the army for three years. Such a requirement is called a "draft." A man could avoid the draft by sending someone else in his place. Certain people were exempted, including owners of 20 or more slaves. This led to complaints of "a rich man's war but a poor man's fight."

The North was slower to use a draft. To encourage volunteers, several states offered bounties, or payments, of $100 or more to men who volunteered. But in March 1863, the North also started a draft. All men over 20 and under 45 had to serve unless they hired a substitute or paid the government $300.

The draft laws in both North and South aroused opposition. In 1863, riots occurred in several Northern cities to protest the draft. In New York City, opposition to the draft combined with prejudice against blacks and economic problems to create the worst disturbances. White men resented being compelled to fight to free blacks who might then compete for their jobs. In the Draft Riots of July 1863, mobs in New York went on a rampage, burning buildings, looting, and killing. More than 100 people, most of them blacks, died in four days of rioting. Army troops were rushed from the battlefield to put down the riot.

Women and the War

In both North and South, mothers, wives, sisters, and other women did what they could to support the men at war. They suffered terrible anxiety about the safety of their loved ones serving as soldiers. Women, both black and white, wondered whether they would ever see their men again.

With men away at war, women back home in both the North and the South took on new responsibilities. They became teachers, factory and mill hands, office workers, and sales clerks. In the South, women took over the management of many plantations. Women also performed many tasks that directly helped the armies. They rolled bandages, wove blankets, and made ammunition. Women collected food, clothing, and medicine for the troops, and raised money to buy supplies.

The most important work women performed during the war was nursing. Previously, nursing had been an exclusively male profession. At first, many doctors—also all men—opposed using women as nurses in military hospitals. The doctors thought women were too delicate for such work and felt it was improper for women to take care of the bodies of strange men. Strong-minded women disregarded these

"Nothing that I had ever heard or read had given me the faintest idea of the horrors witnessed here."

Kate Cummings, Confederate nurse, after the Battle of Shiloh, April 1862

Clara Barton (1821–1912)

Clara Barton was born in Oxford, Massachusetts, into a farming family. She taught school for a while in New Jersey and then went to Washington, D.C., to work in the U.S. Patent Office.

Barton was a strong-willed and determined person. After the First Battle of Bull Run in July 1861, she advertised on her own for materials to aid the wounded. She received such a great response that she organized an agency to distribute the supplies. The next year, she began serving as a nurse on the battlefield. For several years after the war, she ran an official search for missing soldiers.

Barton then went to Europe and worked for the International Red Cross in the Franco-Prussian War. After she returned to the United States, she established the American Red Cross in 1881 and was its director until 1904.

During the Civil War, thousands of wounded men on both sides received care in makeshift hospitals. They were cared for by men and women who worked bravely both on the battlefields and nearby.

objections. In the North, Dorothea Dix organized large numbers of women to serve as nurses in hospitals near the battlefields. Another Northern leader was Clara Barton, who later founded the American Red Cross. In the South, Sally Louisa Tompkins established a hospital in Richmond, and she was made a captain in the Confederate Army.

The War and the Economy

The Civil War strained the economies of both North and South. The North, with its greater resources, was able to cope much better. Both sides raised money by increasing taxes and selling bonds. The North raised more than $2 billion, mainly by selling war bonds that paid high interest. The South raised over $700 million.

All kinds of new taxes were imposed. For the first time, Americans had to pay taxes on their income when, in 1861, Congress passed an income tax in the North. At first, the Confederacy requested money from the states. When that did not provide sufficient funds, it started an income tax in 1863. But neither borrowing nor taxes brought in enough money, so both North and South simply printed paper money. The Northern paper money was called "greenbacks" because of its color. The Confederacy issued $1.5 billion in paper money, more than twice the amount the North printed.

Prices rose faster than wages in the North during the war, causing hardship for working people. This contributed to the tensions that erupted into events such as the Draft Riots of 1863. However, the Northern economy boomed as industry and agriculture responded to the needs of the war with new, more efficient methods of production and organization. Railroad construction increased, as did production of coal, iron, and clothing. The armies' need for a steady supply of food helped farmers prosper.

The Southern economy suffered far more than that of the North. Most of the actual fighting occurred in the South, where farmland was overrun and railroad lines were torn up. By the end of the war, large portions of the South lay in ruins. In addition, the North's blockade helped cause severe shortages of essential goods. Food became scarce, and hungry

Opposition to the War

Both the Union and Confederate governments faced opposition to their war efforts. When the war started, Northern Democrats divided into two groups. One generally supported the war policies of the Lincoln administration. The other group, the "Peace Democrats," was sharply critical and accused Lincoln of being a dictator. Peace Democrats favored negotiating with the Confederacy and tried to win support among voters in the North by appealing to antiblack feelings. Supporters of the war called the Peace Democrats "Copperheads," after the poisonous snake.

Lincoln and other Republicans suspected some Copperheads of being disloyal to the Union. The president sometimes arrested critics he thought were interfering with the war by, for example, discouraging men from enlisting in the army. The people arrested were made subject to military, not civilian, law. This deprived them of certain constitutional rights. Several times, Lincoln suspended the constitutional right of habeas corpus. This right guarantees an accused person a speedy trial on a specific charge.

There was also opposition to the war in the South. President Davis and the Confederate generals at times found it necessary to suspend habeas corpus and hold people without trial.

This $20 bill was issued by the Confederate government in 1861. The Confederates printed large amounts of paper money during the Civil War. But as inflation roared through the South, the bills had little worth.

people rioted in Atlanta, Richmond, and other cities. Inflation—a general rise in prices—was worse in the South. A bag of salt, sold for $2 before the war, cost $60 in some places in the South by 1862. Overall, prices in the South increased 900 percent over the course of the war. In the North, prices increased only 80 percent.

The Draft in America

In America's colonial period, there were laws requiring men to join local militia, but most had been dropped by the time of the American Revolution. The Civil War was the first time the draft, or conscription, was widely used in the United States to obtain soldiers. But a draft has been used several times since then. When the United States entered World War I in 1917, it established local draft boards to recruit soldiers for the military. The first time conscription was used in peacetime was in 1940. That was shortly before America got involved in World War II, when millions of American men were drafted.

In 1948, even though it was peacetime, the United States again began drafting men into the armed forces. Since then, draftees have fought in the Korean War and the Vietnam War. During the Vietnam War, the inequalities of the draft system were much criticized by the antiwar movement. Congress ended the draft in 1973 and today the United States has all-volunteer armed forces.

5

The Union Wins the War

In the fall of 1862, President Lincoln had removed General George McClellan from command of the Army of the Potomac because he wanted a general who would fight more aggressively. But it was some time before Lincoln found a general who could match the South's Robert E. Lee. Under Lee, the Army of Northern Virginia seemed unbeatable.

Fredericksburg and Chancellorsville

At the end of 1862, Union General Ambrose E. Burnside faced Lee at Fredericksburg, Virginia. Burnside's army was far larger, but the Confederates were entrenched on hills behind the town. Repeated attacks by the Yankees on December 13 failed with heavy losses. In tears at his failure, Burnside resigned the command.

He was replaced by Joseph E. Hooker. Hooker rebuilt the army, and in late May 1863, he moved it to Chancellorsville, a few miles west of Fredericksburg. Before he could mount a major attack, however, Lee and the Rebels struck. Boldly dividing his smaller army into groups, Lee won another thrilling victory. But the battle had heavy casualties. The Confederates lost 13,000 men, more than 20 percent of their total; the North lost 17,000, about 15 percent.

Despite his heavy losses, which included the brilliant General "Stonewall" Jackson, Lee thought it was a good time to move north. Perhaps another victory, this time on Northern soil, would persuade Britain and France to recognize the independence of the Confederacy. Maybe the North would even give up the fight.

General Robert E. Lee was a force to be reckoned with. He inspired tremendous trust in the soldiers of the Confederate Army, even though they were often outnumbered. His leadership encouraged his men to several victories against seemingly impossible odds.

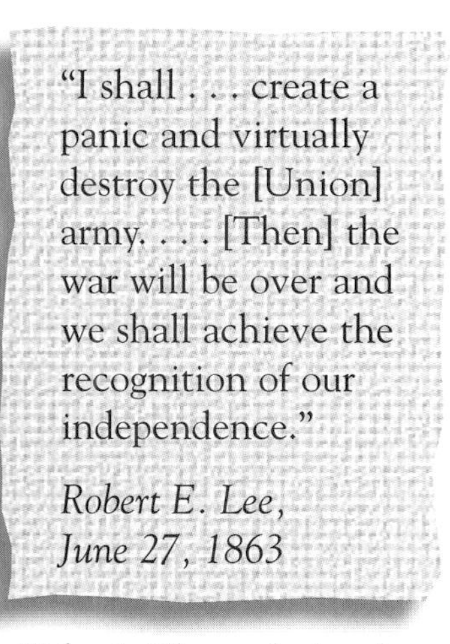

"I shall . . . create a panic and virtually destroy the [Union] army. . . . [Then] the war will be over and we shall achieve the recognition of our independence."

Robert E. Lee, June 27, 1863

Pickett's Charge during the Battle of Gettysburg was a brave but doomed effort on the part of the Confederates. As the men advanced toward Union lines, they were completely unprotected. Wave after wave of soldiers kept coming, opening themselves to direct fire from the opposing army.

The Battle of Gettysburg

Confederate President Davis ordered troops from other parts of the Confederacy to come to Virginia and reinforce Lee's army. In June 1863, with 75,000 men, Lee moved north. Confederate spirits were high.

Meanwhile, Union General Hooker wanted to move on Richmond. Lincoln, however, urged him to attack Lee's army and destroy it. When Hooker began making excuses for not attacking, Lincoln replaced him with George C. Meade.

The Confederates arrived in Pennsylvania toward the end of June and assembled near the town of Gettysburg. One of Lee's generals, Ambrose Hill, ordered some of his men to enter the town in search of shoes and saddles, which the Confederates badly needed—reportedly there was a store of them in Gettysburg. In the town, they met Union soldiers under General John Buford, and fighting began. A major battle started on July 1, 1863, and lasted for three days. About 90,000 Union soldiers faced 75,000 Confederates. On the first day, the Confederates drove the Union forces out of Gettysburg. The Yankees took up strong positions on high ground south of the town. On the second day, furious Rebel attacks failed to drive them off.

Lee was convinced one more attack would break the Union line. On the third day, he sent three divisions, totaling between 12,000 and 15,000 men, into battle under General George Pickett. Pickett's forces charged repeatedly into the center of the Yankee lines. Each time, they were driven back, with many captured, wounded, or killed. By the end of the day, only half of Pickett's men were still able to fight. Lee knew the battle was lost. The next day, the Confederates painfully began making their way back to Virginia.

Union General Meade was satisfied with the Union victory. Lincoln, however, was deeply upset that, once again, the Union army had let Lee's army get away. Still, Gettysburg was a great Union victory. Never again would the Confederates seriously threaten the North. The total number of casualties in the battle was staggering. More than 3,000 Union men were killed and about 20,000 wounded. The Confederates lost more than a third of their army: Nearly 4,000 were killed and 24,000 wounded.

"I tried to ride over the field but could not, for dead and wounded lay too thick to guide a horse through them."

A Union officer, Battle of Gettysburg, July 4, 1863

"We had them in our grasp. We had only to stretch forth our hands and they were ours. And nothing I could say or do could make the Army move."

Abraham Lincoln, July 14, 1863

The Tide of Battle Turns

A great battle on the Mississippi River took place at the same time as the fighting at Gettysburg. Vicksburg, in the state of Mississippi, faces the river from a high bluff. Still in Confederate hands, the town prevented the North from controlling the entire river. For several months, Union forces under Grant had been laying siege to it. Finally, on July 4, 1863, the town surrendered. Now the North could control the entire Mississippi. The states of Texas and Arkansas were cut off from the rest of the Confederacy.

After Grant captured Vicksburg, he and General William T. Sherman won another important victory at Chattanooga, Tennessee, in November 1863. The way was now clear for a Union invasion of Georgia. The Confederate defeats at Gettysburg, Vicksburg, and Chattanooga were a turning point in the war. Although the war continued for two more terrible years, the Confederacy never again won a major battle.

The Gettysburg Address

On November 19, 1863, a ceremony was held at Gettysburg to dedicate a cemetery for the soldiers who died in the battle there. President Lincoln and other dignitaries were invited to speak. Lincoln's brief Gettysburg Address is among the greatest speeches ever made. It beautifully expresses what Lincoln thought the war had come to mean:

"Fourscore and seven years ago our fathers brought forth on this continent a new nation, conceived in liberty and dedicated to the proposition that all men are created equal.

"Now we are engaged in a great civil war, testing whether that nation or any nation so conceived and so dedicated, can long endure. We are met on a great battlefield of that war. We have come to dedicate a portion of that field, as a final resting place for those who here gave their lives that that nation might live. It is altogether fitting and proper that we should do this.

"But, in a larger sense, we can not dedicate—we can not consecrate—we can not hallow—this ground. The brave men, living and dead, who struggled here, have consecrated it, far above our poor power to add or detract. The world will little note, nor long remember what we say here, but it can never forget what they did here. It is for us the living, rather, to be dedicated here to the unfinished work which they who fought here have thus far so nobly advanced. It is rather for us to be here dedicated to the great task remaining before us—that from these honored dead we take increased devotion to that cause for which they gave the last full measure of devotion—that we here highly resolve that these dead shall not have died in vain—that this nation, under God, shall have a new birth of freedom—and that government of the people, by the people, for the people shall not perish from the earth."

Dead soldiers lie on the battlefield of Gettysburg.

In early 1864, Lincoln made Grant the commander of all the Union armies. Grant had a simple plan. In Virginia, the Army of the Potomac would try to capture Richmond, Virginia, and crush Lee's army. Sherman would drive from Tennessee to Atlanta, Georgia. If the plan succeeded, the Confederacy would be destroyed. Grant was very well aware that the North had far more men and supplies than the South. He intended to use them, even at the price of huge losses.

Grant put his strategy into effect in May 1864. His large army of 115,000 men smashed into Lee's army of 75,000 Rebels in a series of battles—the Wilderness, Spotsylvania, and Cold Harbor—near Richmond. Each time, the Confederate lines held. But the Union armies behaved differently from previously, as Grant ordered them to renew the attack immediately. In June, Grant swung south of

Victories at Fredericksburg in late 1862 and Chancellorsville in early 1863 gave hope to the Confederates. But in 1863 the Union won major victories at Gettysburg and Vicksburg. In 1864, the larger Union forces under Grant put relentless pressure on the Rebels in Virginia.

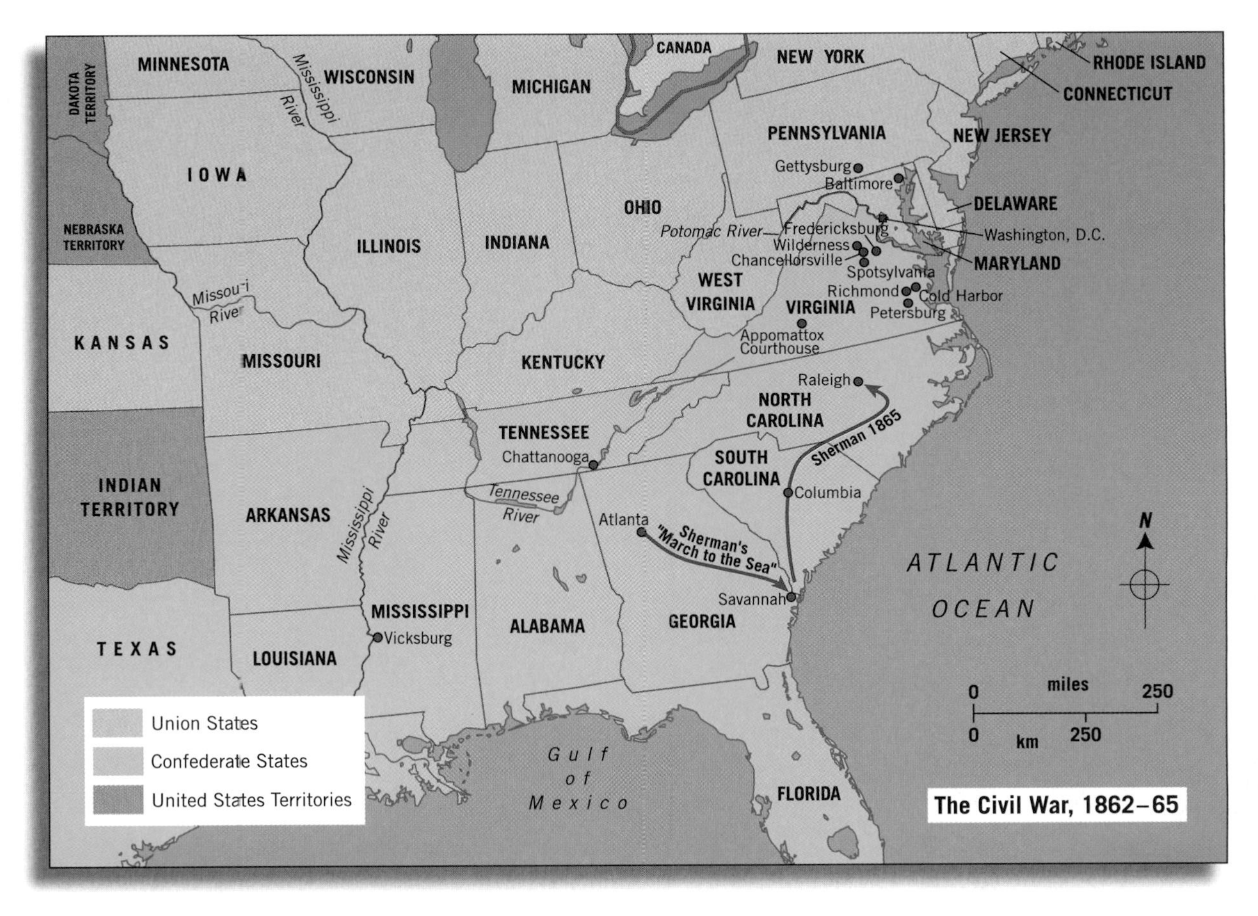

"I propose to fight it out along this line if it takes all summer."

Ulysses S. Grant, Spotsylvania, Virginia, May 11, 1864

"We are not only fighting hostile armies, but a hostile people, and must make old and young, rich and poor, feel the hard hand of war."

William T. Sherman, Memoirs

Richmond and attacked Petersburg, a key railroad junction. If it fell to the Union, Richmond would be cut off from the rest of the Confederacy. Each side dug long trenches. From June 1864 until April 1865, when the Confederate troops withdrew, Petersburg was under siege.

The battles in May and June 1864 cost the North more than 60,000 men. Critics called Grant a "butcher." But he was determined to continue and Lincoln supported him. They both knew that, eventually, Lee's army would not be able to withstand the pressure.

General Sherman carried out the other part of Grant's strategy. Starting from Tennessee in the spring of 1864, Sherman's army advanced toward Atlanta and entered it on September 2. Then Sherman began his historic "March to the Sea" to Savannah, Georgia. His army abandoned its supply lines and lived off the land it passed through. After taking what it needed, the army destroyed nearly everything in its path. A Yankee soldier said, "a tornado . . . could not have done half the damage we did." Sherman captured Savannah in December 1864.

General Sherman (center right, by cannon) poses with his staff after the capture of Atlanta, Georgia. Union forces entered Atlanta in September 1864 after a month-long siege. Within a few months, Sherman had also taken Savannah. On the way there, his troops caused millions of dollars worth of damage to Georgia property.

The Union Generals

Like their Confederate counterparts, many top Northern generals were trained at West Point and served in the Mexican War. Three of the most outstanding of these were George B. McClellan, Ulysses S. Grant, and William Tecumseh Sherman.

George B. McClellan (1826–85) was born in Philadelphia. When the Civil War began, McClellan became a general in Ohio and then head of the Army of the Potomac. McClellan was a skilled organizer and administrator. But he developed an exaggerated sense of his own importance and resented having to take orders from Lincoln. After Lincoln removed him from command, McClellan got involved in Democratic party politics. He was defeated as the Democratic presidential candidate in 1864 against Lincoln. McClellan served as governor of New Jersey from 1878 to 1881.

Ulysses S. Grant (1822–85) was born in Ohio. After the Mexican War, his army career was unsuccessful and he resigned in 1854. When the Civil War started, Grant rejoined the army. Grant's victories in the West and his willingness to attack hard and keep fighting impressed Lincoln. The North's victory in the Civil War made Grant a great hero. He was elected president in 1868 and served two terms. Grant was an honest man but a poor political leader. His presidency was marked by scandal and corruption.

William Tecumseh Sherman (1820–91) was also born in Ohio. After a period in the 1850s as a banker in California, he became head of the Louisiana Military Academy. In the Civil War, Sherman served under Grant at Shiloh, Vicksburg, and Chattanooga. Then he led the Union invasion of Georgia and the famous "March to the Sea." Despite his reputation for cruelty, Sherman told a military class, "I am tired and sick of war. . . . War is hell." When Grant became president in 1869, Sherman succeeded him as the chief U.S. general. Sherman retired from the army in 1884.

The 1864 Election

Also in 1864, an important event took place in the North. A presidential election was held in all the states loyal to the Union. There were two main candidates. The Republicans renominated Lincoln and tried to broaden their appeal by choosing Andrew Johnson, a pro-Union former Democrat from Tennessee, for vice president. The Democrats chose George B. McClellan, whom Lincoln had fired as general, for president and picked Congressman George Pendleton of Ohio for vice president.

"I am going to be beaten and unless some great change takes place, badly beaten."

Abraham Lincoln, talking about the presidential election, August 1864

The main issue, of course, was the war. Lincoln was criticized from all sides. Within his own party, some thought he was not doing all he should to punish the South and end slavery. The Democrats, on the other hand, wanted to make peace with the South as soon as possible. They attacked Lincoln for prolonging the war so he could free the slaves.

During the summer of 1864, Lincoln's chances looked bad. Grant's army was suffering enormous losses and the North was tired of the war. As Lincoln hoped, however, a great change did take place. When Sherman captured Atlanta in September, the North's mood altered. At last, the end of the war was in sight. Lincoln won the election and was inaugurated for the second time on March 4, 1865. In his Inaugural Address, he pledged to fight the war to a successful conclusion.

On April 4, 1865, President Lincoln came to Richmond, Virginia, with his 12-year-old son, Tad. They were cheered through the streets by crowds of newly freed blacks. One elderly black man took off his hat and bowed to the president. With tears rolling down his cheeks, he said, "May God bless you." Lincoln removed his own hat and bowed in return.

The End of the War

The end came little more than two months later. After capturing Savannah, Sherman had turned north. In early 1865, his army tramped through South and North Carolina, continuing its savage destruction. Sherman intended eventually to come up to Virginia and there join in the attack against Lee.

Lee had been in Virginia since the previous summer, desperately defending Petersburg and Richmond. His army had shrunk due to casualties, desertion, sickness, and hunger. Finally, on April 2, 1865, the Confederate lines broke. Lee sent word to Jefferson Davis that Richmond had to be abandoned. By nightfall, the defenders, government officials, and many residents had fled. Those who remained set fire to much of the city.

Union forces, including a cavalry troop of black soldiers, entered Richmond the next day. Lee had moved his army west of the city. He hoped somehow to link up with a small Confederate force that was trying to stop Sherman in North Carolina. But soon, Lee realized his situation was hopeless and let Grant know he was ready to surrender.

Lee and Grant met on April 9, 1865, in the small village of Appomattox Courthouse, Virginia, to arrange for the Confederate surrender. Grant's terms were generous. The Confederate soldiers had to lay down their arms, but they were free to go home. They could keep their horses so they could "put in a crop to carry themselves and their families through the next winter." When Grant got back to his headquarters, he ordered three day's worth of food for 25,000 men to be sent to Lee's troops. Several days later, the Confederate forces in North Carolina surrendered to Sherman. Jefferson Davis was captured in Georgia on May 10. The Civil War was over.

General Lee (seated left) surrendered to General Grant (seated right) in April 1865, bringing the Civil War to a close. It was an unconditional but reluctant surrender. Before the meeting, Lee said to an aide, "There is nothing left for me to do but go and see Grant, and I would rather die a thousand deaths."

Just five days after Lee surrendered to Grant, President Lincoln was assassinated by John Wilkes Booth at Ford's Theater. After firing the fatal shot, Booth shouted out, "Sic temper tyrannis! The South is avenged!" The Latin words are the state motto of Virginia, and mean, "Thus always to tyrants."

"Now he belongs to the ages."

Secretary of War Edwin M. Stanton after Lincoln's assassination, April 1865

Assassination

The North's jubilation was spoiled, however, by the murder of President Lincoln. On April 14, 1865, the president was shot in the head while watching a play in Ford's Theater in Washington, D.C. He died the next morning. The murderer was an actor named John Wilkes Booth. Booth, Maryland-born, was mentally unstable and a fanatical Confederate. He had assembled a group of conspirators to help him in his plan to avenge the defeat of the Confederacy.

The group also plotted to kill Vice President Johnson, General Grant, and Secretary of State William H. Seward. In a separate incident on the same night, Seward was stabbed and seriously wounded, but he recovered. The plot against the others was not carried out, and Johnson was sworn in as president on April 15, 1865.

After the shooting of Lincoln, Booth escaped and by late April had reached Port Royal, Virginia. On April 26, he was captured in a barn near the town and killed. Four of his fellow conspirators were later hanged and four others imprisoned.

Evaluating the Civil War

Why did the North win the war? Historians have debated this question extensively. Several reasons have been

Richmond, Virginia, stands in ruins after its days as the Confederate capital. Everywhere in the South, the Civil War had left its devastating mark. Large areas of cities and smaller towns were reduced to rubble. Factories and fields were completely destroyed. Railroad lines were torn up, and countless houses burned or looted.

suggested. As we have seen, the North had greater resources of men, equipment, and raw materials. During the course of the war, Lincoln proved to be a more effective leader than Jefferson Davis. By the end of the war, the North also had military leaders at least as able as those in the South. Also, the states' rights philosophy in the South made it difficult for the Confederacy to wage war effectively, because the states were unwilling to give up their power to a central Confederate government. And many slaves did what they could to weaken the South's war effort.

But things still could have turned out differently. At several times, the South came very close to winning. What if Rebel armies had won the Battle of Antietam in September 1862? Lincoln might not then have issued the Emancipation Proclamation, and Britain and France might have recognized the Confederacy as an independent nation. Or, suppose Lee had succeeded at Gettysburg in 1863. He might then have marched on Washington or Baltimore. Perhaps Lincoln might have lost the presidential election in 1864 to McClellan. With McClellan as the Union leader, the Confederacy might possibly have gained independence through a negotiated peace.

One thing we know for sure. The Civil War was the bloodiest conflict in American history. More than 620,000

"With malice toward none, with charity for all . . . let us strive on to finish the work we are in, to bind up the nation's wounds, to care for him who shall have borne the battle and for his widow and his orphan, to do all which may achieve and cherish a just and lasting peace among ourselves and with all nations."

Abraham Lincoln, Second Inaugural Address, March 4, 1865

soldiers died. That is more than all the deaths in America's other wars combined. In addition, many civilians died in the South. And the destruction in the South was so great that not until 1880 did the region again produce the amount of crops it had grown in 1860.

Bitter feelings toward the North among the defeated Southerners lasted for generations. But for the nation as a whole, the idea that a state could leave the Union had been defeated. The federal government had won a victory over individual states and appeared more powerful than ever. Perhaps most important, after the Emancipation Proclamation ended slavery in the South, close to 4 million black Americans living in Southern states were no longer slaves. Now they were free people.

Presidential Assassinations

Abraham Lincoln was the first president assassinated, or murdered, in office. Since then, there have been three other presidential assassinations.

President James Garfield was shot on July 2, 1881, by Charles Guiteau, an unstable man with failed political ambitions. Garfield died on September 19. William McKinley was shot on September 6, 1901, by a political extremist named Leon Czolgosz, and died on September 14. John F. Kennedy was shot on November 22, 1963, and died the same day. His assassin was probably Lee Harvey Oswald, an ex-Marine who was himself murdered two days later.

There have also been several attempted presidential assassinations. On January 30, 1835, an insane man fired two pistols at President Andrew Jackson, but both guns misfired. A few weeks before his inauguration, on February 15, 1933, President Franklin D. Roosevelt narrowly escaped being shot by Giuseppe Zangara, an unemployed bricklayer. The president-elect was unharmed, but others in his car were hit and Mayor Anton Cermak of Chicago was killed. On November 1, 1950, two Puerto Rican nationalists attempted to kill President Harry Truman. In September 1975, President Gerald Ford escaped assassination by deranged women on two occasions. And President Ronald Reagan was wounded by the insane John Hinckley, Jr., on March 30, 1981.

6

Reconstructing the Nation

After the Civil War, the United States went through a time called the Reconstruction period. The term reconstruction means "rebuilding," and this rebuilding took several forms. One concerned the states of the defeated Confederacy. A society that had been based for generations on the work of slaves now had to adjust to the end of slavery. How would these 11 Southern states be brought back into the Union?

A second aspect of Reconstruction concerned the millions of black Americans who had formerly been slaves. Now, as "freedmen," what place would they take in American society? Abraham Lincoln in his Gettysburg Address had spoken of "the great task remaining . . . that this nation, under God, shall have a new birth of freedom." Would the United States now accomplish the task Lincoln had set before it? In the North as well as the South, black people had never enjoyed equality with whites, and most Americans doubted this could happen. During Reconstruction, Americans faced these difficult problems and challenges.

> "Slavery is not abolished until the black man has the ballot [vote]."
>
> *Frederick Douglass, May 1865*

Policies toward the South

Even before the Civil War ended in spring 1865, President Lincoln had started to make plans for Reconstruction. Lincoln hoped that by offering generous terms to Southerners, he could persuade them to end their rebellion.

Lincoln offered his "10 percent plan" in December 1863. When 10 percent of

The black people of the South, such as this group of recently freed slaves, now had their liberty. But what would their future be?

the voters in a Southern state had taken an oath pledging loyalty to the Union and accepted the abolition of slavery, they could organize a new government for their state. By 1865, Louisiana, Arkansas, and Tennessee had formed new governments loyal to the Union.

However, an important group in Congress, known as the Radical Republicans, felt the 10 percent plan did not do enough. Among the leaders of the group were Senator Charles Sumner of Massachusetts and Representative Thaddeus Stevens of Pennsylvania. The Radical Republicans were deeply committed to the ideal that all Americans should be equal under the law. They and their supporters wanted especially to make sure that black men had the right to vote. (At this time, no women, black or white, were allowed to vote.)

"[The federal government should] revolutionize Southern institutions, habits, and manners. . . . The foundations of their institutions . . . must be broken up and relaid, or all our blood and treasure will have been spent in vain."

Thaddeus Stevens, ca.1864

The Radical Republicans also believed the South should be harshly punished. They wanted a majority—not just 10 percent—of Southerners in a state to swear loyalty before the state could rejoin the Union. Moreover, to be active in the new governments, Southerners must take an "ironclad" oath that they had never aided the Confederacy. Some Radical Republicans wanted to break up the great plantations of the South and give the lands to the freedmen and to poor whites who had been loyal to the Union. Lincoln indicated he might back the right to vote for at least some of the freedmen. He and the Radical Republicans were discussing their differences shortly before Lincoln was assassinated in 1865.

The new president, Andrew Johnson, required only that Southerners accept the abolition of slavery. Once former Confederates pledged loyalty to the Union, they could get all their property, except for slaves, back. Johnson had little interest in the rights of the freedmen, and he did not want to expand the powers of the federal government in order to protect those rights.

By the end of 1865, every Southern state had met Johnson's requirements and elected members of Congress. The Republican majority in Congress was very alarmed by

The Radical Republican Leaders

Thaddeus Stevens (1792–1868) was born in Vermont and moved to Pennsylvania after graduating from Dartmouth College in 1814. He became a successful lawyer and, as an abolitionist, frequently defended fugitive slaves in court for free. Stevens also became part owner of an ironworks in Pennsylvania.

Stevens was elected to the House of Representatives as a Whig in 1848 and served until 1853. He left Congress in disgust over the slavery issue, but later helped found the Republican party in Pennsylvania and returned to Congress in 1858. Stevens led the movement to impeach President Johnson in 1868.

Charles Sumner (1811–74) was from Massachusetts and graduated from Harvard Law School in 1833. He was opposed to war and slavery, and was one of the founders of the Free-Soil party.

Sumner became a senator for Massachusetts in 1851. He, along with Stevens, was a founder of the Republican party, and was reelected to the Senate in 1857, 1863, and 1869 as a Republican. However, between 1856 and 1859, he was unable to attend Congress because of the injuries he received in the Senate during an attack by Representative Preston Brooks. When he returned to government, Sumner fought for the rights of black people and against white control of the South during Reconstruction.

Johnson's policies. They were worried that little was being done to protect the freedmen. The Republicans also feared that the return to power of the former Southern leaders would revive the Democratic party in the South. If that happened, the Republicans might lose their control of the federal government. The Constitution gives Congress the authority to judge the qualifications of its members. Using that authority, the Republican-led Congress refused to accept the new senators and representatives from the South.

Life for the Freedmen

All over the South, freedmen rejoiced in their newly gained liberty. Black families that had been separated by their

> "We most earnestly desire to have the disabilities under which we have formerly lived removed; to have all the oppressive laws which make unjust discriminations on account of race or color wiped from the statutes of the State."
>
> *Address at the Convention of Colored People of North Carolina, October 1864*

owners during slavery made great efforts to reunite themselves. Blacks submitted petitions and held meetings and parades to assert their rights as Americans. The freedmen demanded the right to vote and the end of laws and regulations that discriminated against them. Often these efforts were led by blacks who had served in the Civil War, since many had learned to read and write while in the army.

The freedmen were helped by the Federal Bureau of Refugees, Freedmen, and Abandoned Lands, formed in 1865. Known simply as the Freedmen's Bureau, it assisted former slaves by providing food and medical care. It also helped set up schools that were staffed largely by young men and women from the North who came to the South to support equal rights for freed blacks.

The freedmen's main task was to find a way of supporting themselves. In some areas during the war, they had been able to take over lands that had been abandoned by plantation owners. The Freedmen's Bureau and, in some cases, the Union Army, helped them do this. By the end of the war, about 10,000 families of former slaves had settled on lands in Georgia and South Carolina. Thousands more looked forward to obtaining some of the land they had previously worked as slaves.

Recently freed slaves crowd into the Freedmen's Bureau in Memphis, Tennessee, at the start of Reconstruction. They came to seek food rations, medicine, and hope for their future in the South.

Even before the end of the Civil War, slaves had taken over abandoned plantations. At this plantation, which had belonged to Confederate General Thomas Drayton, former slaves began to harvest the cotton for themselves. But during Reconstruction, President Johnson ordered the army to force blacks off the lands they had so recently obtained.

President Johnson's Reconstruction policy, however, enabled many white Southerners to recover their old plantations. Without their own land, many blacks throughout the South could obtain work only by laboring on the farms of their former owners for very low wages.

In 1865 and 1866, the new Southern governments passed laws called the "Black Codes." In some respects, these laws reflected that blacks were no longer slaves. They recognized marriages between blacks and also allowed blacks to testify in court and own certain kinds of property. But in other ways, the Black Codes made blacks second-class citizens. They were not allowed to vote and they could not own guns. In most states, the codes made it difficult for blacks to work except as farmers and servants. All sorts of other restrictions were placed on them, and if they violated the restrictions, they could be fined. If they could not pay the fines, they were forced into labor for whites.

Congressional Reconstruction

Congress passed several bills in 1866 in an attempt to help freedmen. One new law strengthened the powers of the Freedmen's Bureau. It gave the Bureau temporary authority over abandoned lands in the South, and the right to bring people to trial if they were depriving blacks of their civil rights. Another law, the Civil Rights Act, declared blacks to be United States citizens, and prohibited states from violating blacks' rights in various ways. Congress also passed a law that enabled anyone, including freedmen, to acquire ownership of public land in the South by cultivating it for five years.

President Johnson vetoed the Freedmen's Bureau bill and the Civil Rights Act. He said they were unconstitutional because they affected the Southern states that were still not represented in Congress. But Congress passed both bills over Johnson's vetoes, making this the first time in American history that important legislation had become law despite a president's veto.

The Radical Republicans then persuaded Congress to pass the Fourteenth Amendment to the Constitution and send it to the states for ratification. The amendment defined U.S.

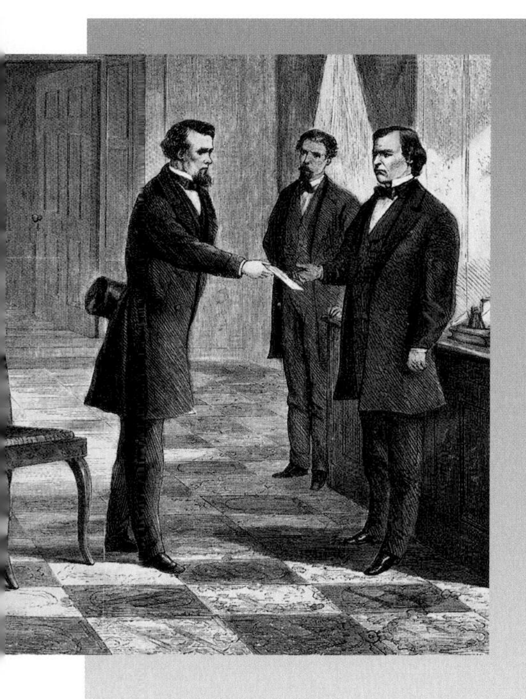

President Johnson receives a summons to his impeachment trial in 1868.

Andrew Johnson (1808–75)

Andrew Johnson was the seventeenth president of the United States. Born in Raleigh, North Carolina, into a very poor family, Johnson was largely self-educated. He moved to Tennessee in 1826 and entered the House of Representatives in 1843. Later, he was elected governor and then a U.S. senator. Johnson did not oppose slavery, but he did not believe a state could secede from the Union. During the Civil War, President Lincoln appointed Johnson military governor of Tennessee. Then, in 1864, Lincoln chose him to run for vice president to help his reelection chances. Johnson became president when Lincoln died on April 15, 1865.

Johnson quarreled bitterly with the Radical Republicans in Congress over Reconstruction policy and narrowly escaped being removed from office. Johnson tried but failed to get the Democratic nomination for president in 1868. Shortly before his death in 1875, Tennessee again elected him to the U.S. Senate.

Soldiers occupy a street in New Orleans, Louisiana, during the time of Reconstruction. The Reconstruction Acts of 1867 said the governments of ten former Confederate states were illegal, and placed military commanders in charge of them. Troops were posted all over the South to protect the new rights of black people.

citizenship to include blacks and it banned discriminatory laws like the Black Codes. But it could not go into effect unless three-quarters of the states ratified it, and the amendment was rejected in all the former Confederate states except Tennessee.

In spite of this setback, Radical Republicans gained strength in Congress in the 1866 elections. They now decided to impose their concept of Reconstruction on the South. Congress passed a group of Reconstruction Acts, starting in March 1867. Johnson vetoed them, but Congress overrode his vetoes. Under the new laws, all of the South except for Tennessee was divided into five districts. Each was put under the control of a U.S. Army general. The generals would see to it that, in each state, new laws were adopted. These laws guaranteed black men's right to vote and took away the vote from former Confederates. Each state also had

"All persons born or naturalized in the United States . . . are citizens of the United States and of the State wherein they reside. No State shall make or enforce any law which shall abridge the privileges or immunities of citizens of the United States; nor shall any State deprive any person of life, liberty, or property, without due process of law; nor deny to any person within its jurisdiction the equal protection of the laws."

Fourteenth Amendment to the Constitution, Section 1, 1868

It was the responsibility of the military governments under the Reconstruction Acts to register black voters in the South. Once they were given the opportunity to vote in elections, black Southerners voted overwhelmingly for Republican candidates.

to ratify the Fourteenth Amendment. Only then would their representatives be permitted back into Congress. In June 1868, Alabama, Georgia, Florida, Louisiana, North Carolina, and South Carolina were readmitted to Congress. In September, however, Georgia was put back under military rule when it expelled black members from its state legislature.

The Fourteenth Amendment was ratified in 1868. But in some parts of the South, blacks still had difficulties exercising their right to vote. And at this time, blacks were not permitted to vote in many *Northern* states. Wisconsin, Minnesota, Connecticut, Nebraska, New Jersey, Ohio, Michigan, and Pennsylvania all had laws preventing blacks from voting. In early 1869, Congress proposed the Fifteenth Amendment, which guaranteed the vote to all black men. The Fifteenth Amendment was ratified in 1870. Congress insisted that Virginia, Mississippi, Texas, and Georgia ratify it before they could be represented in Congress. By July 1870, all four states had agreed to the terms and been readmitted.

The Impeachment of President Johnson

President Johnson and Congress had repeatedly clashed over Reconstruction policy, and now Congress wanted to make sure Johnson did not interfere with administration of the Reconstruction Acts. Accordingly, it passed the Tenure of Office Act in March 1867. This law required the president to obtain the Senate's approval before he could dismiss any official who had been appointed with the Senate's consent. When Johnson then fired Secretary of War Edwin Stanton, the Senate refused to approve the dismissal. The president, believing the Tenure of Office Act to be unconstitutional, fired him anyway.

In February 1868, Congress began impeachment proceedings against Johnson. The House of Representatives voted by a large majority to impeach Johnson, but the Senate failed by one vote to convict him. Seven Republicans joined with the Democrats in voting against conviction. Removing the president from office, they thought, would upset the proper constitutional balance between the legislative and executive branches of government. Johnson remained in office, a very weak president, until his term ended on March 4, 1869.

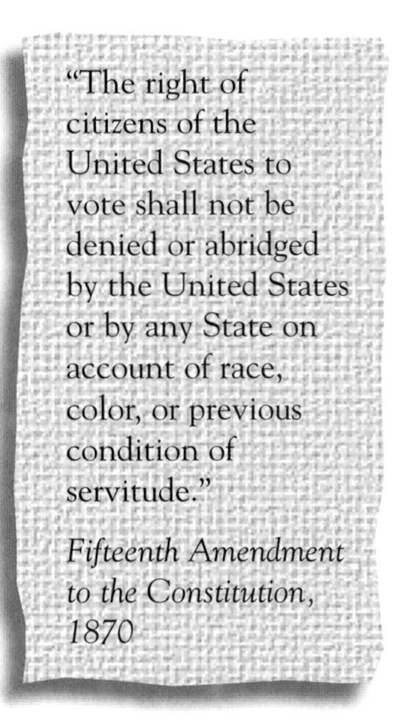

"The right of citizens of the United States to vote shall not be denied or abridged by the United States or by any State on account of race, color, or previous condition of servitude."

Fifteenth Amendment to the Constitution, 1870

Black Reconstruction in the South

The state governments established in the South during Reconstruction were different from any previous ones. These governments were dominated by the Republican party. The Black Codes were repealed and, for the first time, blacks could take part freely in public life. In several Southern states, they even made up a majority of the voters. Republican political clubs enrolled blacks, hoping to win their votes.

Blacks played an important role in state and local affairs during Reconstruction, when hundreds of them served as government officials. Sixteen were elected to the U.S. House of Representatives, and two to the U.S. Senate. No black, however, was elected governor, although three did become lieutenant governors.

Many Southern whites were opposed to the new governments and unfairly criticized them as corrupt and inept. They claimed black officials were just ignorant field hands. In fact, the Reconstruction governments were no more corrupt than other governments in the United States at that time, and they accomplished a great deal. They made a start at modernizing the

The first black members of Congress, shown here, included the first senator, Hiram Revels (seated, far left). The others, all representatives, were (left to right) Benjamin Turner, Robert De Large, Josiah Walls, Jefferson Long, Joseph Rainy, and R. Brown Elliot.

Carpetbaggers brought education to black adults and children all over the South, as in this school run by the Freedmen's Bureau.

Scalawags and Carpetbaggers

Several groups of whites joined with blacks in running and supporting the new governments. One group consisted for the most part of Southerners who had never owned slaves. Another, wealthier group, was made up of Southerners who wanted the South to work with Northerners so the South could enjoy the kind of economic growth that existed in the North. A third group, Northerners who had moved South after the war, often served as governors and congressmen.

Some Southern whites called the pro-Republican Southerners "scalawags" —an old Scotch-Irish term for a runty animal—and said they were traitors to their race. They called the Northerners "carpetbaggers," because of the small cloth suitcase some carried, and accused them of coming South just to make money. While some did come out of greed, most were educated people like teachers and lawyers or former Union Army officers. They came south to help with education, legal problems, and rebuilding the shattered region.

South's economy by investing in manufacturing industries. They constructed roads and rail lines and built hospitals and other facilities for people in need. In some states, medical care and legal advice were made available to poor people.

The Reconstruction governments also greatly expanded the South's tiny public school systems. Previously, education for blacks was illegal in most places in the South. Nearly all the new schools were segregated by race, but now more Southern children, both black and white, were able to attend school than ever before.

During Reconstruction, blacks also worked hard in their families and communities to build new homes and better lives for themselves. In addition to education, religion became part of the effort blacks made to improve themselves. Religion had always been important to slaves, and now the freed blacks built their own churches and religious organizations. Black Baptists, Presbyterians, and Methodists founded new churches, and existing black religious groups experienced enormous growth. The African Methodist Episcopal Church had only 20,000 members in 1856, before the Civil War. By 1876, it had 200,000. In 1861, there were 150,000 black Baptists in the South; by 1870, there were 500,000. Church ministers served not only as religious leaders, but often became political leaders of the black communities as well. Hiram Revels, a United States senator in 1870–71, was also a Methodist minister.

"If I never does do nothing more while I live, I shall give my children a chance to go to school, for I considers education the next best thing to liberty."

A black Mississippian, 1869, quoted in Ordeal by Fire *by James McPherson*

Impeaching the President

Impeachment is the method the Constitution provides for removing a president and other federal officials from office if they have committed "Treason, Bribery, or other high Crimes and Misdemeanors." The Constitution says that the House of Representatives can bring impeachment charges against the official. The issue then goes to the Senate, which acts as the jury in an impeachment trial. When a president is impeached and tried, the Chief Justice of the Supreme Court presides over the Senate.

No president has ever been removed from office by impeachment. Only two presidents have been brought to trial before the Senate: Andrew Johnson in 1868, and Bill Clinton. The House of Representatives voted to bring charges against President Bill Clinton on December 19, 1998. Clinton was accused of giving false testimony and other crimes relating to matters in his personal life. On February 12, 1999, however, the Senate acquitted Clinton of the charges.

In July 1974, President Richard Nixon was threatened with impeachment. He was accused of obstruction of justice and concealment of illegal acts in the Watergate scandal. It seemed likely that he would be convicted, but Nixon resigned as president on August 9, 1974, before the entire House could vote on his impeachment. He is the only U.S. president to have resigned.

7

The End of Reconstruction

> "THE GREAT and paramount issue is: SHALL NEGROES or WHITE MEN RULE NORTH CAROLINA?"
>
> *A North Carolina newspaper, quoted in* Ordeal by Fire *by James McPherson*

In the South, both the Reconstruction governments and blacks in their local communities accomplished a lot. But they were not able to make real and lasting changes in the power structure of the South. Within a few years, the Reconstruction governments were overturned by whites opposed to equality for blacks, and the nation's leaders lost interest in the cause of racial equality.

No 40 Acres and No Mule

When the Civil War ended, many freedmen had hoped to acquire land. As independent farmers, they felt they would be able to support themselves and their families. This hope was reflected in the slogan "40 acres and a mule." Black people hoped to acquire land to farm and draft animals to help with the farmwork. But for the most part, the hope was never realized. As we have seen, proposals in Congress to divide up the lands of the great Southern plantations were defeated and President Johnson's policies allowed former Confederates to regain their property. Freedmen could settle on the public lands that were available, but many lacked the resources to move their families and buy the seeds, tools, and animals necessary to farm the land. Most of the state governments did not have the money to help them.

> "Every colored man will be a slave, and feel himself a slave until he can raise [his] own bale of cotton and put [his] own mark upon it and say this is mine!"
>
> *A black army veteran, quoted in* Ordeal by Fire *by James McPherson*

By 1880, only about 20 percent of Southern blacks owned the land they worked. The majority worked instead for white landowners under conditions only a little better than slavery. Some were paid very low wages, while others worked under arrangements called "sharecropping." The sharecropper leased land in return for paying the landowner a share of the crops raised. Sharecroppers often ended up hopelessly in debt to the landowners for farm equipment and other necessary supplies.

Sharecropping was the only option for many Southern blacks after the Civil War. But it was a system that made it almost impossible to prosper. Sharecroppers ended up with little or nothing after meeting the demands of landowners.

The "Redeemers"

The Republican-led state governments in the South were bitterly opposed by most former slave owners. They wanted to return, as much as possible, to the days when they were the most powerful people in Southern society. Most of these conservative whites organized their return to power within the Democratic party. They called the process the "Redemption" of the South and thought of themselves as the "Redeemers." To achieve their goal, they needed to do two things. First, they had to get the support of poor whites. Second, they had to find a way to drive out of public life the people—both black and white—who supported Republican policies.

Former slave owners took advantage of the resentment many poorer whites felt against the freedmen. The new schools and other improvements made by the Reconstruction governments were helping both whites and blacks. In spite of this, appeals to racial prejudice were successful in turning many whites against the Republicans.

The Ku Klux Klan

To frighten blacks and their white supporters, organizations practicing violence or threatening violence sprang up in the South during the 1860s. The most important of these organizations was the Ku Klux Klan, or KKK. Klan members came from all segments of white Southern society and by 1868 were operating in many states. The Klan's main aim was to frighten people from voting Republican, and to achieve this they used terrible violence. The Klan threatened, beat, and even murdered people. In Colfax, Louisiana, for example, the KKK killed dozens of blacks and two whites after a disputed election in 1873. Black churches and schools were burned down, and teachers whipped.

Now that the Southern states had functioning civilian governments, U.S. Army troops stationed there earlier to

Nathan Bedford Forrest (1821–77)

Nathan Forrest was a Confederate general and leader of the Ku Klux Klan. He was born in Tennessee, the son of a farmer and blacksmith; his family moved to Mississippi in 1834. By the time he was in his 20s, Forrest had engaged in several bloody fights with pistols and knives. He was fiery and quick to avenge what he considered an insult to his honor. Forrest prospered in local businesses and as a slave trader. Eventually, he became the owner of a large plantation with many slaves.

In the Civil War, Forrest became a distinguished cavalry leader. Wounded several times, he personally killed 30 Union soldiers. Troops under his command committed the massacre of black soldiers at Fort Pillow, Tennessee, in April 1864.

Two Ku Klux Klansmen of the 1800s.

After the war, President Johnson granted Forrest a pardon for his activities as a Confederate. For a time, Forrest cooperated with the Freedmen's Bureau in arranging contracts for black workers. Forrest joined the Klan in 1867 and soon became its leader, the Grand Wizard. He made the Klan a feared force in the South. In 1868, Tennessee's Republican governor, William Brownlow, said he intended to destroy the Klan in the state. Forrest responded that he would fight and "raise 40,000 men in five days." Brownlow backed down and resigned.

enforce Reconstruction laws had been withdrawn from many areas. So the ability of soldiers to prevent racial violence was limited. Congress passed new laws in 1870–71 giving the remaining soldiers special authority to protect black voters and clamp down on Klan activity. Hundreds of Klan members were arrested, although all-white juries convicted very few of them. The laws eventually did succeed in breaking up the Klan, but the damage had been done. Fewer blacks came out to vote in elections and fewer whites were willing to be seen as friends of blacks.

Policies and Problems

In the midst of all this turmoil, Ulysses S. Grant had been elected president in 1868. Southern blacks, who were now allowed to vote, cast 450,000 votes in Grant's favor, probably giving him his victory. Grant, a supporter of the Radical Republicans, defeated the Democrat Horatio Seymour, a former governor of New York.

Grant was reelected in 1872, beating newspaper editor Horace Greeley. During his second term, however, national leaders and the public gradually lost their enthusiasm for reforming the South. Many of the old Radical Republican leaders in Congress had retired or died by the mid-1870s. The new national leaders now had other issues to occupy their attention.

The Republicans were committed to stimulating American economic growth, and passed much new legislation to do so. Private railroad companies received government money to expand their lines. River and harbor improvements were financed by the government. Many of the taxes first imposed during the Civil War were continued to pay for these programs. And the economy did grow. For example, steel production boomed, increasing by nearly 20 times between 1870 and 1880. However, this rapid economic expansion benefited rich investors more than average citizens. A severe economic depression, or downturn, began in 1873. The depression lasted several years, during which time 15 percent

The Republican and war hero Ulysses S. Grant was twice elected president. Although Grant was personally honest, his presidency ran into trouble in his second term as more and more scandals in his administration came to light.

of the nation's workers became unemployed and thousands of farmers were ruined.

Meanwhile, scandals involving high officials in the Grant administration and the Republican party came to light. Grant himself was not involved, but the scandals overshadowed his presidency. The depression and the scandals caused a dramatic shift in public opinion.

The Democrats Gain Control

In 1874, the Democrats regained control of the United States House of Representatives for the first time since before the Civil War. This occurred just as Southern white voters were uniting behind the Democratic party and the Redeemer policies. The state governments, too, were returning to Democratic leadership. Virginia and Tennessee were "redeemed" in 1869, North Carolina and Alabama in 1870. Other states followed in the 1870s. The Republicans decided relying on blacks for support was not a good strategy. They were tired of the seemingly endless struggle to protect the rights of blacks in the South.

What happened during Mississippi's election in the fall of 1875 showed the new Republican attitude. Pro-Democratic, antiblack groups paraded with weapons. They broke up Republican meetings and openly threatened blacks and their white supporters. Hundreds of blacks were killed in riots. Governor Adalbert Ames appealed to President Grant for U.S. troops, but Grant refused to send them. He and his advisers thought there was little they could do in Mississippi and feared losing support elsewhere. In the election, Democrats gained control of the state.

The federal courts also gave no help to black people. The Supreme Court interpreted the Fourteenth and Fifteenth Amendments and the civil rights laws in ways that made them useless for protecting blacks' rights. By 1877, the Democrats were in control of all the Southern states except Florida, Louisiana, and South Carolina.

The End of Reconstruction

The Reconstruction period is considered to have ended in 1877. In the 1876 presidential election, Democrat Samuel B. Tilden won a popular majority over the Republican Rutherford B. Hayes. But the electoral votes of three Southern states—Florida, South Carolina, and Louisiana—and of Oregon were disputed. Without them, Tilden lacked the majority of votes he needed to be elected. Congress set up a special committee to settle the election disputes. It did so by awarding all the disputed electoral votes in question to Hayes. That gave Hayes an electoral majority of one vote.

The three Southern states were still occupied by federal troops. To get the Democrats in Congress to accept the decision on the vote dispute, the Republicans promised to withdraw remaining troops from the South. They also promised to appoint at least one Southerner to the Cabinet and to give support for improvements in the South. The Southern states, under their Democratic governments, would now be allowed to do as they pleased. In practice, this meant the end of the attempt to guarantee blacks in the South full political and civil rights.

"The whole public are tired out with these annual autumnal outbreaks in the South, and the great majority are now ready to condemn any interference on the part of the [federal] government. . . . Preserve the peace by the forces in your own state."

U.S. Attorney General Edward Pierrepont to Mississippi Governor Ames, who had appealed for federal military help in Mississippi, September 14, 1875

Blacks' Right to Vote Denied Again

The South now became a one-party region. Within the Democratic party, various political and economic groups of whites struggled to gain power. For a time, rival white factions tried to win black votes, and corruption spread as black votes were bought and sold. But while they fought among themselves, Southern whites could always agree on one thing: They thought themselves superior to blacks.

In the late 1800s, black people began to migrate to other areas to get away from the injustices of life in the South. This print shows four scenes of a journey made by black refugees from Louisiana and Mississippi. The scene at the top shows their arrival in Kansas, where they hoped to acquire their own land and live free of prejudice.

During the 1890s, the Southern states, starting with Mississippi, began once again to deny blacks the right to vote. The states used seemingly "legal" regulations, a practice that had actually begun earlier in the border states. For example, voters might be required by law to pay a tax, or to pass reading and writing tests. They might have to prove that they owned property. These requirements could have prevented poor whites as well as black people from voting, and so to avoid this they were linked to a "grandfather clause." If a potential voter could show that his grandfather had voted, then he wouldn't have to pass any of the other requirements. Of course, most blacks' grandfathers had been slaves who never voted. So, as the majority of blacks could not pass the other requirements either, they were not allowed to vote.

A Segregated Society

Gradually, in the late 1800s and early 1900s, the South made itself into a racially segregated society. That is a society where the blacks and whites are kept apart, and in such a way that whites have superiority over blacks. "Jim Crow" is the name applied to this kind of society in the United States. The term comes from the name of a character in a popular song-and-dance act. Under Jim Crow, not only was it made very hard for blacks to vote, but laws placed them in inferior positions in all major aspects of life. Schools, playgrounds, restaurants, and public transportation were all segregated. So were hospitals, churches, and cemeteries. The ones set aside for blacks were almost always not as good as the ones for whites. In some places, courts even had separate Bibles for black witnesses to swear upon.

In 1896, the Supreme Court ruled that segregation did not violate the Fourteenth Amendment. The Court said in the case of *Plessy v. Ferguson* that segregation was lawful as long as the "separate facilities were *equal*." Of course, they hardly ever were equal, but that was very difficult to prove. Social customs as well as laws enforced black inferiority. Blacks were expected to behave meekly around whites. Just as they had done as slaves, they had to address whites respectfully. Whites, on the other hand, could call a black of any age "boy" or "girl."

Violence against blacks became a part of Southern life. One form of violence was lynching. A mob would seize a black man thought guilty of a crime and kill him, usually by hanging him from a tree. Often before being hanged, the black was tortured, and parts of his body might be cut off and given out as souvenirs. More than 7,500 blacks were lynched between 1884 and 1914. Many of them had committed no crime.

And what of the North? While Jim Crow was taking hold in the South, conditions in the North were better for blacks but far from ideal. Belief in the equality of whites and blacks had never been widely held there either. By the middle of the Civil War, Northerners generally had come to feel that slavery was wrong. But that was very different from thinking

"We are taxed without representation. . . . We obey laws; others make them. We support state educational institutions, whose doors are virtually closed against us. We support asylums and hospitals, and our sick, dumb, or blind are met at the doors by . . . unjust discriminations. . . . From these and many other oppressions . . . our people long to be free."

Charles Harris, black Union Army veteran and former Alabama state legislator, August 28, 1877

"If one race be inferior to the other socially, the Constitution of the United States cannot put them upon the same [level]."

U.S. Supreme Court, Plessy v. Ferguson

that blacks and whites should have the same opportunities in all aspects of life. There had been fierce opposition in some Northern states to the Fifteenth Amendment, which in 1870 gave all black men the right to vote. This helps explain why the federal government in the 1870s lost its commitment to black rights in the South. Public opinion in the North just did not believe firmly in that commitment. Many Northern communities did have laws banning discrimination in public facilities like trains and restaurants. However, these laws were not always enforced and discrimination was common.

The Different Ku Klux Klans

The first Ku Klux Klan, or KKK, was founded in Pulaski, Tennessee, in 1866. The Klan was at first a social club of Confederate Army veterans, but quickly became an organization whose goals were to keep blacks from voting and help conservative white Democrats return to power. Members rode through the countryside at night wearing hooded costumes of white sheets and robes. They intended to frighten blacks into thinking they were the ghosts of dead Confederates. Klan members burned homes, schools, and churches and even murdered blacks and their white supporters.

U.S. government authorities broke up the Klan in the 1870s. Another organization with the same name was founded in Georgia in 1915. It spread into the North and Midwest as well as through the South. This second Klan was anti-Catholic, anti-Jewish, and anti-immigrant as well as anti-black. In the early 1920s, it achieved a membership of several million people, many of whom joined for social reasons. Membership quickly declined, however, when the Klan's terrible activities were publicized and several of its leaders were convicted of violent crimes. By 1930, there were believed to be only about 9,000 members.

When the civil rights movement began in the South in the 1950s, terrorist groups calling themselves the KKK reappeared. They used violence in an attempt to intimidate blacks and civil rights workers. Eventually, the Federal Bureau of Investigation (FBI) and other law enforcement agencies effectively put an end to most Klan activity. Yet the Ku Klux Klan still exists today and incidents of KKK violence occur occasionally.

Conclusion

The Civil War changed forever the character of America. The United States was now clearly a single, unified nation. No state had the right to secede. The war changed America in other ways, too. It led directly to the abolition of slavery. And, partly due to the war, the United States would soon become one of the greatest economic powers in the world. This was because, in its need to win, the North had developed and organized economic resources as never before.

The war left a legacy of courage, heroism, and suffering that would long be remembered. In the following years, Americans would come to appreciate the accomplishments of people on both sides of the conflict. In memory, history books, and novels, and later in movies and television programs, their stories would live on. The deeds of people such as Lincoln, Lee, Grant, Jackson, Hiram Revels, and Sojourner Truth have not been forgotten. The achievements and sufferings of the men of Pickett's Charge, the 54th Massachusetts Regiment, and countless other ordinary soldiers and civilians are told and retold.

The Reconstruction era that followed the Civil War, however, left a more troubled heritage. America had been founded on the ideal of the Declaration of Independence that "all men are created equal." Lincoln in the Gettysburg Address had rededicated the nation to "a new birth of freedom." The war brought freedom to black Americans. But it did not bring equality in either the South or the North. Within a few decades of the Civil War's end, the South became a segregated, Jim Crow society. Not until the civil rights movement started in the 1950s did things change significantly. Then, Lincoln's Civil War vision of "a new birth of freedom" truly began to be realized.

Glossary

abolitionism The movement to end slavery.

administration The managing of public affairs or business, or the group of people who carry out the management.

amendment An addition to a formal document—for example, to the United States Constitution.

annexation The act of taking ownership of another nation or adding territory to a nation.

arsenal A store of weapons and ammunition.

authority The power to make decisions and rules, or the people who have that power.

blockade To cut off an enemy area—for instance, by preventing ships and supplies from going in or out of ports.

bond A certificate promising repayment to a person who has lent money.

cavalry Soldiers who fight on horseback.

constitution The basic plan and principles of a government.

delegate The person chosen to represent others at a meeting or in making decisions.

Democrats The political party founded in the 1820s and in which Southerners who supported states' rights were very powerful for many years.

draft A system requiring people by law to serve in the armed forces.

economic To do with the production and use of goods and services, and the system of money that is used for the flow of goods and services.

executive The branch of government that enforces laws.

export To send something abroad to sell or trade. An export is also the thing that is sent, such as tobacco or cotton.

Fifteenth Amendment The amendment to the Constitution, ratified in 1870, that aimed to protect the right of black people to vote.

Fourteenth Amendment The amendment to the Constitution, ratified in 1868, that aimed to protect the civil rights of black people.

habeas corpus The right of an arrested person to have a speedy trial on a specific charge.

impeachment The process by which Congress can remove public officials from office.

import To bring goods into a country. An import is also the thing that is brought in, such as tea or cloth.

legislative To do with lawmaking, or the branch of government that makes laws.

legislature An official group of people with the power to make laws.

plantation A farm where crops, such as tobacco or sugarcane, are grown, and where the work is done by large teams of workers. In the past, these workers were often slaves.

policy A plan or way of doing things that is decided on, and then used in managing situations, making decisions, or tackling problems.

popular sovereignty The political idea that voters in a territory should decide for themselves whether to allow slavery.

radical A person who favors distinct political, economic, or social changes or reform.

ratify To approve. For example, the U.S. Senate must ratify treaties before they can go into effect.

Rebels Southerners or Confederate soldiers during the Civil War.

repeal To undo an earlier decision.

Republicans The political party founded in 1854 to oppose the expansion of slavery.

secede To leave the Union. The act of leaving is called *secession*.

sectional Something divided into sections, such as the political interests of people in different regions of a country.

segregation The policy of keeping people from different racial or ethnic groups separate. It usually means one group has fewer rights than another.

states' rights The powers and rights belonging to the states, particularly the right to oppose acts by the federal, or national, government that the states thought unconstitutional.

strategy The overall military plan for dealing with an enemy or a conflict.

unconstitutional An action or law not authorized by the Constitution.

veteran A person who served for a long time at a job, particularly in the military, or who served on a particular campaign or expedition.

Yankees Northerners or United States soldiers during the Civil War.

Time Line

1820–21	Missouri Compromise.
1831	Nat Turner slave rebellion.
1846–48	Mexican War.
1846	Wilmot Proviso proposed.
1850	Compromise of 1850 passed.
1852	*Uncle Tom's Cabin* published.
1854	Kansas-Nebraska Act
	Republican party founded.
1856	"Bleeding Kansas."
1857	Dred Scott Supreme Court decision.
1858	Lincoln-Douglas Debates.
1859	John Brown's raid at Harper's Ferry.
1860	Abraham Lincoln elected president.
1860–61	11 Southern states secede from Union and form Confederate States of America.
April 1861	Civil War begins with firing on Fort Sumter.
July 1861	First Battle of Bull Run.
March 1862	Clash of *Monitor* and former *Merrimac*.
April 1862	Battle of Shiloh.
June–July 1862	Seven Days Battles.
August 1862	Second Battle of Bull Run.
September 1862	Battle of Antietam.
October 1862	Battle of Perryville.
December 1862	Battle of Fredericksburg
January 1, 1863	Emancipation Proclamation goes into effect.
May 1863	Battle of Chancellorsville.
May–July 1863	Siege of Vicksburg.
July 1863	Battle of Gettysburg
November 1863	Battle of Chattanooga.
September 1864	General Sherman captures Atlanta.
November 1864	Lincoln reelected president.
November–December 1864	Sherman's "March to the Sea."

April 9, 1865	General Lee surrenders to General Grant at Appomattox.
April 14, 1865	President Lincoln assassinated.
April–May 1865	Last Confederate forces surrender.
December 1865	Thirteenth Amendment ratified.
1865–66	Southern states enact Black Codes.
1866	Ku Klux Klan founded.
April 1866	Civil Rights Act.
June 1867	Fourteenth Amendment sent to states for ratification.
March 1867	First Reconstruction Act.
1867–68	"Black Reconstruction" governments formed in Southern states.
February –May 1868	Impeachment of President Johnson.
July 1868	Fourteenth Amendment ratified.
November 1868	Ulysses S. Grant elected president.
1869–1877	Democratic governments come to power in the South.
March 1870	Fifteenth Amendment ratified.
November 1872	Grant reelected president.
September 1873	Severe economic depression begins.
November 1876	Hayes-Tilden election dispute.
1877	Rutherford B. Hayes elected president. End of Reconstruction.

Further Reading

Biel, Timothy Levi. *Life in the North during the Civil War* (Way People Live Series). San Diego, CA: Lucent, 1996.

Black, Wallace B. *Slaves to Soldiers: African-American Fighting Men in the Civil War* (First Books Series). Danbury, CT: Franklin Watts, 1997.

Chang, Ina. *A Separate Battle: Women and the Civil War* (Young Readers History of the Civil War Series). New York: Lodestar, 1991.

Collier, C. and J. L. Collier. *The Reconstruction Era, 1864–1896* (Drama of American History Series). Tarrytown, NY: Marshall Cavendish, 1999.

Haskins, Jim. *The Day Fort Sumter Was Fired On: A Photo History of the Civil War*. New York: Scholastic, 1995.

Meltzer, Milton, ed. *Lincoln in His Own Words*. San Diego, CA: Harcourt, 1993.

Naden, Corinne J. and Rose Blue. The House Divided Series, 4 vols. Austin, TX: Raintree Steck-Vaughn, 2000.

Reger, James P. *Life in the South during the Civil War* (Way People Live Series). San Diego, CA: Lucent, 1997.

Websites

Abraham Lincoln Online – Everything about Honest Abe: speeches, photographs, a quiz of the month.
http://www.netins.net/showcase/creative/lincoln.html

Civil War Soldiers & Sailors System – A database of 235,000 records for soldiers serving in the U.S. Colored Troops during the Civil War.
http://www.itd.nps.gov/cwss/

The Civil War Home Page – Maps and information about all the battles of the Civil War.
http://www.civil-war.net/battles.html

The Civil War and Reconstruction (1850 to 1877) – A collection of biographies, documents, and army unit information concerned with the Civil War and Reconstruction.
http://quaboag.k12.ma.us/civwar.html

Bibliography

Foner, Eric. *Reconstruction: America's Unfinished Revolution, 1863–1877*. New York: Harper, 1988.

Franklin, John Hope. *From Slavery to Freedom: A History of Negro Americans*. Fifth edition. New York: Knopf, 1980.

Henretta, James A., et al., *America's History*. New York: Worth, 1993.

McPherson, James. *Ordeal by Fire: The Civil War and Reconstruction*. New York: Knopf, 1982.

______. *Battle Cry of Freedom: The Civil War Era*. New York: Oxford University Press, 1988.

______. *What They Fought For, 1861–1865*. Baton Rouge, LA: Louisiana State University Press, 1994.

Morris, Richard B., ed. *Encyclopedia of American History*. Seventh edition. New York: HarperCollins, 1996.

Index

Page numbers in *italics* indicate maps; numbers in **bold** indicate illustrations.